W9-ABA-022

When the Birds Stopped Singing

Living with the Wounds of War: Personal Essays

Clemens Loew

Cover sculpture "my father" by Clemens Loew

Copyright © 2014 Clemens Loew
All rights reserved.

ISBN: 1496180623
ISBN 13: 9781496180629

In honor and memory of Oskar Neustein, Karola Neustein, and Andrzej Loew, whose extraordinary courage and devotion enabled me to live the life depicted in this collection of essays.

Table of Contents

Acknowledgments

Mindy Lewis, for her inspirational classes and guidance.

Laura Sewell, for her meticulous attention and gentle hands throughout the editing process.

The nuns and priest of the convent outside Warsaw, whose courage in the face of death sheltered me as if I were Christian.

Roger Monaco, for his friendship.

Nina Singer, for being the "sista" I never had.

The Boys: Drs. Dave Altfeld, Jim Fosshage, Ken Frank, and Henry Grayson, for their brotherhood.

Anja Behm, German-born, whose friendship helped me to better understand the complexities of post-war German-Jewish relations.

The Chicago Loews: Uncle ("Unc"), Aunt Rita, and their children, Jonathan, Andrea, Josh, and Jennifer Melissa, who provided a loving family and home when I most needed it.

Jody Davies, whose compassion and understanding enhanced my life and distanced me from the abyss.

Jennifer Alexandra and Shannon, my loving children, who from their beginning brought meaning, purpose, and light to my life.

Aline Sosne, whose love and laughter open new frontiers as we share moments of our past and present, and dreams of the future. I thank her for her courageous, late-inning editing.

Author's Note

Having lived as a child through times of Nazi violence, I am familiar with loss and terrifying uncertainty, and have witnessed gritty heroism. This is a memoir about my mother's fierce genius for survival and deep love for me. It is the story of love and hope found in new relationships, and of my struggle to give meaning to the madness I experienced and witnessed and that lingers in me as an adult. I acknowledge that along with the privilege of survival comes the obligation to live one's life to its fullest and honor those who did not survive.

The Apron

Years ago, when I was about seven, I hid in the shadows cast by my mother and grandmother. It was dusk, and they were arguing in a dimly lit apartment I had never seen before. Their urgent whispers cloaked me in a heavy, dark blanket of secrets and fear. I felt dazed and lost.

Moments earlier, the three of us had climbed a flight of stairs and tiptoed down the hallway to this apartment, like criminals. When we found the right door, Grandmother knocked so gently that I hardly heard her. But soon, someone approached from within, pressing an eye against the peephole. A short woman wearing a long, brown bathrobe opened the door and waved us in. We passed through the partial opening as quietly as hot air rising to the ceiling. The woman, surprised to see us at this hour, was very fidgety, and she spoke nervously. Hearing the fearful pleading in my mother's voice, she agreed that we could stay the night.

"But you must leave before daylight," she insisted, and looked to Mother for agreement.

Mother nodded and hugged her friend. "Yes, I understand," she said. "Thank you, thank you."

The friend brought out a blanket and spread it on the floor. She motioned my grandmother to the couch. Mother and I were to sleep on the floor. I lay down, but I stayed in my clothes because the blanket was itchy and smelled from mothballs.

I couldn't sleep. I tried to figure out exactly what day and what time it was. I was having trouble remembering everything that had happened that day.

It probably had been earlier that afternoon, while my mother was at work, that I had been sitting silently on the floor watching my grandmother cook at the black wood-burning stove in the corner of our new room. She was wearing a long, loose dress with her old, white apron wrapped around her and was carefully cutting the chicken and vegetables to add to the liquid simmering on the stove to make chicken soup. The air, warmed by the fire and scented by her cooking, was as soothing to me as my mother's lullabies. For a moment I forgot where I was: in a room that she and my mother had recently rented on the ground floor in the back of another woman's house. They had to show the landlady documents— false, of course—to prove that we were Christians before she let us inside. We had lived in this room several weeks, or perhaps it was months; it's all a blur now.

We were hiding, under disguised names, in eastern Poland's cultural city of Lvov. That was in the fall of 1942, about a year after I had watched, through the second-floor window of the house my grandfather built, the first German soldiers invade the street below. Although I had been warned by my parents about the war, seeing the soldiers' high boots and black helmets and the swastikas on their arms frightened me beyond anything I could have imagined. They came in September, the month of my birthday, into my hometown,

Stanisławów, south of Lvov. I remember because my mother was planning a party for me that same month.

The day the Nazis came, my mother pushed me away from the window and told me to be quiet. I had overheard my parents talking about people disappearing and never returning, and I knew now that my family and I were being hunted, too. I didn't know exactly why; I only knew that it was connected to the fact that we were Jews. From that moment, I knew I would have to hide to stay alive.

My party never happened. Within days of the invasion, we—my parents, my mother's parents, and I—together with the other Jews on the block, were herded by soldiers with pointed rifles into a well-guarded ghetto. There was no way to leave, except on the back of a Nazi truck. The ghetto was established on the other side of my hometown. Nevertheless, it was my father's ingenuity that got me, my mother, and my grandmother the Catholic papers that would enable us to escape the ghetto. To insure authenticity, he asked a sympathetic priest for the name of a boy in his parish who had recently emigrated out of our town. My father then gave that name to the forger to make up the papers. The name on my new birth certificate said "Klemak Nowicki."

During those last few days in the ghetto, my parents taught me to "forget" my real name and remember only the new one. My mother and father called me by my new name, Klemak, and told me that if someone called me by my real name I had to ignore it.

My father, so tall and slim, with light brown hair and a receding hairline, tested me over and over. I sensed an urgency in his firm voice that actually made me feel protected. I knew he was teaching me something that could save my life.

"What's your name?" he asked, looking into my eyes.

"K-k-klemak," I stuttered.

It was very strange and difficult to be someone else, but my father repeated these exercises until I felt like the false name was my own. I wondered who Klemak was. What did I need to make up to make myself become Klemak? I played with the name and made up stories about him. The stories felt like lies. But then, maybe they weren't.

Finally, my mother, grandmother, and I said goodbye to my father and grandfather, leaving them behind in the ghetto, with plans to go to Lvov with our false names and papers. My father reassured me that they would meet us in Lvov in a few days, as soon as they could arrange for their escape. We left in the middle of the night, going through a checkpoint, where the guard, who had been bribed with jewelry, let us out.

A week or two later, in the room Mother and Grandmother rented in Lvov, while we were still waiting for Father and Grandfather to join us, Grandmother glanced out the window and saw a black car pulling up in front of the house. Two men in gray suits got out. Alarmed, she quickly removed the pot from the fire and put it on the floor.

She grabbed my hand. "We have to get out!" she whispered. "The police are here. We have to find your mother!"

Her tension, urgency, and the dreaded word "police" sent shudders through my body. Darkness descended over the entire room, snuffing out the cozy aroma and soothing spirit. Grandmother pushed me to the back of the house, heaved the window open, climbed through it, and dropped to the ground. Then she told me to do the same while she held her arms out to catch me. We ran down the street, with her pulling me after her. There was no time to think about what we were leaving behind.

It was late afternoon, with the reddish sun lighting the street from the left side behind the four-story buildings. The sun drew square shadows on the left and illuminated the granular stone buildings on the right. Between the shadows were slices of brightness formed by the alleys.

We moved at a varied pace, between the dark and light places, trying not to arouse suspicion. I wished it were nighttime. Night, like fog, attracted me because it hid all my secrets and weaknesses.

I saw two strangers watching us, their heads turning and tracking our movements. I imagined eyes everywhere, behind windows, on rooftops, hidden in the doorways and alleys, all straining to figure out why this woman with the boy was rushing so much. Where were they going? I imagined the eyes asking themselves. Who were they running from? And why did she still have her apron on? I pictured them solving the puzzle, and all the eyes relaxed. That's when I became even more nervous. Because they must have figured it out: the woman and the boy were Jews, running from the Nazis.

When we came to the busy area of town, we slowed down. Grandmother was breathing hard. Her eyes narrowed, and she scanned everyone around us. Her forehead was beaded with sweat; she patted it down with her shirtsleeve. It was only then that she noticed the apron. She quickly took it off, rolled it up, and slipped it under her arm.

When we reached the trolley stop, Grandmother whispered, "We have to catch your mother as she gets off the trolley, before she goes home. If not, she is sure to get caught." I stiffened and tried not to tremble. I noticed that my pants were torn and that I had scraped my leg climbing out of the window. It hurt, but I didn't complain. I was too distracted to care about the wound. I just needed more air; I felt my chest rising and falling, and my mouth was wide open. I wiped sweat off my face with my forearm.

We stood in silence. My grandmother held my hand so hard that it hurt. The longer and harder she squeezed, the more frightened I became. As one trolley after another stopped and let out its passengers, I carefully watched every person getting off, especially the women. Tall, short, young, and old, I scanned them all. I was searching for something special that would identify my mother at the very first glance, before she walked away from us and headed home. Then I remembered that she always wore a brown beret tilted to the left side of her head. I watched for that. I knew that one of the women had to be my mother.

When I finally saw Mother on top of the trolley steps waiting to get off, I started to run toward her. But Grandmother held onto my hand and jerked me back.

"Walk slowly," she said, quietly looking down at me. "Like normal—one step at a time." When we got close, she let go of my hand, which was hurting from her grasp. I rushed toward Mother and held her as tightly as I could. She kissed her own mother on the cheek, with no hug, as they usually greeted each other. Then, while I stood leaning against her leg, I heard Grandmother tell her in a hush that the landlady must have reported us, and the Gestapo had come. Mother was silent for a moment. She bent over, hugged me, and kissed me on my cheek. As she kissed me, she ran her hand over my hair, stroking my head from my forehead to the back of my neck, something she always did when she was trying to calm me. Or maybe she was trying to calm herself, too.

"I have a friend," she said finally, "who lives nearby. Maybe she will let us stay with her."

"Are you sure?" asked Grandmother.

As Mother and Grandmother continued to talk, their faces looked more worried, and I became even more anxious. I lost track of time. I saw that the sun was leaving us. The lower it sank beyond the edge of what I could see, the more beautiful the light it left behind. The quick disappearance of the sun pleased me. I hoped to have less light on me, so I wouldn't have to worry about the eyes watching us. I thought about my real name, but I was too frightened to even say it in my mind. I felt safer with Klemak, but I wondered when I would get my real name back. I didn't want to forget it completely.

The three of us moved silently along the streets in search of the friend's building. I held Mother's hand as she led the way. Her hand was smooth, and I had a habit of playing with her fingers; it reminded me of the comforting feeling I got when I was younger and held my soft, blue blanket to my mouth.

Mother was very pretty and young, only twenty-five years old. She looked like her mother, except that Grandmother was actually taller and stronger. Mother had a round, fresh face that always looked like she had just washed it with soap and water. The light brown color of her eyes reminded me of warm tea in a clear glass. Her nose was perfectly rounded and small, and she carried herself like someone from an upper-class family. Though I did not appreciate its importance at that time, her cute button nose and aristocratic demeanor were critical to our safety, as they made her look Christian... or at least not Jewish.

I, in contrast, had deep brown eyes and a big nose. My face did not fit my Christian name. When the weather was cool, Mother would wrap a scarf around my face. With my nose hidden, I was supposed to look more like Klemak. I think I did look like him then, but inside I felt ashamed walking the streets as Klemak, as if I belonged in a basement with no windows and no light.

At Mother's friend's apartment, after we were shown the couch and the floor and the friend left the room, Mother and Grandmother argued quietly about who should go back to retrieve the valuables. I lay silently on the floor on the itchy blanket, pretending not to hear their conversation.

We had no bags or suitcases. The only belongings we had with us were the clothes we were wearing and whatever possessions Mother had taken to work with her that morning in her leather handbag. We would need the money and documents that were hidden under the stove in our apartment to move on and find another place in a different town.

Grandmother held in one hand the large, white apron stained with chicken soup and parsley from the meal she had been preparing. I felt cold and scared. I sniffed her apron like an animal. It made me feel warmer, as if I were back home about to eat my favorite food.

"Let me go," Mother said. "I can move faster in and out of the apartment and get what we need."

"No," insisted Grandmother. "Your son is too young to be left without his mother. Anyway, I will be back quickly, before dawn."

Mother turned to find me sitting against the wall in the shadows and looked at me for a long time. After a short silence, she turned to face her mother.

"All right," she said. "But you must be careful. We don't want to lose you. If you see anything suspicious, come back. Don't go in. Do you understand?"

Grandmother found me by the wall, knelt down, and gave me a big kiss on the forehead. She stroked my head from side to side. I put my arms around her. She still smelled good from the food I had not eaten. She said that she'd be back soon, and I believed her. On the way out, I saw her drop the apron on a chair by the door.

I stayed awake on the floor and waited nervously, but hopefully. I never did go to sleep that night. By the next morning, when Mother's friend said we had to move on, Grandmother had not yet returned. I kept waiting, sure she would find us sooner or later. Over time, the sense-memory of her delicious cooking remained sharper than the visual image of my grandmother, which faded as I grew older. Sometimes, even as an adult, I expected my grandmother, and along with her my father and grandfather, to return. I never saw any of them again.

When the Birds Stopped Singing

The nun introduced herself as Sister Leonia. "All the sisters here belong to the Order of Sisters of Maria's Family," she said, looking into my mother's eyes. Sister Leonia was eighteen years old. She had soft blue eyes and a warm smile, with pinkish cheeks. Her head was covered by a white cornette that hid her ears and exposed a pretty and gentle face. A dark blue habit covered the rest of her.

In the spring of 1943, as the young nun was showing us around the convent, I clutched my mother's hand as we stood in the doorway of a large, immaculate hall. The floor glistened from the light shining through the small windows, high on the walls, and ten bunk beds were on each side, evenly arranged about three feet apart, lined up against the walls. Each bed was covered with white sheets, so that from my height, standing at the entrance of the hall, I saw white carpets floating in the air. My mother turned toward me as if to say something, but all I could see were her watery eyes. The Nazi war had been raging in our eastern Poland for two years.

Sister Leonia turned to my silent mother. "What's the matter? Don't you like it here?" "Oh, yes," my mother answered quickly. Her voice stammered. "It's so clean here. It looks so safe. It's more than... than I expected."

The orphanage, a two-story, white stucco building, was located in Otwock, a small town on the eastern side of Warsaw. Green grass surrounded the building, which was framed by a white stone fence. The five-foot wall, with a wrought-iron gate, gave the illusion of safety from the outside world.

My mother wiped her tears with a handkerchief. And after a long pause, she asked, "Will you take my son?" Her voice sounded tired and scared, not like the mother I knew.

Sister Leonia reassured her. "You came highly recommended by our bishop in Warsaw. He asked us to take care of your boy. And we will."

"Did the bishop tell you about us?" my mother asked. I knew that "us" meant that we were Jewish.

"We know about you, and I understand your situation," the nun responded. "We take care of thirty boys. There are two others like your son, also about six years old. We will do whatever we can to keep him safe."

"Oh, thank you, thank you. I am forever indebted to you. God bless you and the bishop."

The sister patted her on her shoulder and asked, "Do you have any baggage for him or anything?"

My mother explained that she had no baggage because she didn't want to look suspicious to the Germans. The sister looked at me with curiosity. She saw what I had already seen in the mirror: a skinny, six-year-old boy with dark hair and eyes, long neck, and a big nose. It was the nose that always gave me away, and I wished that I didn't have it. I had, what one Polish landlady had called, an "unfavorable look," meaning I didn't look Aryan.

I also felt embarrassed about the sister looking at my bulgy clothes. Instead of packing my clothes, my mother had made me wear two of everything—two underpants, two pairs of pants, and two shirts. I also wore two pairs of socks, and they were making my feet sweat inside my brown, ankle-high shoes. I looked down at my shoes to avoid the nun's eyes, hoping she wouldn't find me strange.

The nun's soft voice comforted me. "Don't worry, we will find things for him to wear. As you can imagine, we have limited food and resources, but rest assured that we will treat your son like any other boy here. Now, how can we get in touch with you, and will you be coming to visit?"

"It will be impossible to reach me. It's best that I contact you," I heard my mother say. "But I will visit on Sunday, my day off, as often as I can. Is that all right with you?"

"Yes. Of course. I understand," the nun said, nodding.

My mother pulled me by my hand to a corner for privacy. She bent down and asked me as softly as she could, "Do you like this place? It's clean, and the nuns are friendly, don't you think?"

I nodded, but I didn't listen. To me, her low voice was the sound of distant whispers I couldn't understand. I did not want to be left alone but didn't know what to say or how to say it. My eyes were focused on the haggard man on the wall with his arms outstretched and head hanging down. The naked man, with a cloth over his private parts, was pinned on a cross.

"You'll have to stay here for a bit," my mother continued, "but the nuns will take good care of you. I have to find work. All right?"

She tried to get me to look at her, but I was still gazing at the strange statue.

"We have no other choice," she explained. "But I will try to visit you every Sunday. I will be here. If I don't come one Sunday, it's because I couldn't. You understand?"

I nodded without looking at her.

Then she added, "If anything happens to me," turning my head around to face her, "your uncle will come for you. All right?"

I heard some of what she said, but the rest of her words continued to *whoosh* by my ears as unintelligible whispers. My eyes turned toward the wounded man on the wall, and I began to move the tip of my right forefinger along the edges of my right thumbnail, until I formed a perfect square. I counted the sides: one, two, three, four. And I repeated it over and over again. I don't know how or when I picked up this habit, but it comforted me.

My mother kissed me on the head, said goodbye, and went out the door. I didn't hear the front door close. I focused on the other children coming in from playing outside. Sister Leonia took my hand and showed me my bed, and then, pointing to the bathroom, asked me to take my extra clothes off. The bathroom was empty. It had white tiled walls with three tall, white enamel urinals on the left side. To pee, you had to step on a brick platform in front of the urinals. There were two toilets on the right with no door but a floor-to-ceiling wooden wall separating them. I played it safe and took my clothes off by the toilet. When I finished, she showed me my bed and wooden locker. I put my extra underwear, pants, and shirt into the locker.

That first night, I lay in bed and tried to remember what my mother told me about her visits on Sundays. She'd said "when she could." Did that mean this coming Sunday? Every Sunday? Why wouldn't she be able to visit every Sunday? It was only a short train ride from the center of Warsaw! My head felt hot, and when I closed my eyes, my thoughts bounced around wildly in blotches of many colors. Under the covers, my forefinger was sliding along my thumbnail counting its sides: one, two, three, four.

I tried to figure out what had happened that got me into this strange orphanage, with my mother somewhere in Warsaw. The two of us had been hiding from Nazis under forged Christian birth certificates. We lived in many towns and neighborhoods under false identities. Whenever Mother sensed that the landlord or a coworker were getting suspicious of our true identity, she fled to a different town or place, and we started all over again.

I thought of the last place we had lived together, a room we rented briefly in an apartment building in Lvov, and of my last afternoon there, a few days before I came here. My mother was at work that day. I was playing soccer with five older boys in the courtyard, chasing and kicking the ball back and forth between goalposts marked by pieces of clothing. In the middle of our yelling and screaming, the big, round landlady who managed the apartment building walked out of the side door. I watched her march in a straight line, just like a soldier, in my direction. She had a stern look, and I wondered what I had done. What did she want? We all stopped moving and gazed at this woman swinging her arms.

"Move to the corner, over there!" she shouted at me, and pointed to where she wanted me to go. I did what she asked. She pushed me against the wall with her hate-filled eyes, without touching me. My body shook, not knowing what to expect. Then, standing close, the landlady cast a shadow over me and blocked any escape. All I could see were her thick legs, covered by a brown dress, but I knew the other boys had to be watching. I was six years old. The landlady pointed at my lower body. "Take your pants down!" she demanded with a conviction that her order would be unquestioned.

I stood there frozen, looking straight ahead. I saw grease stains on the bottom of her dress. Then I heard the same voice repeat the order. "Take your pants down!"

I sensed the boys all staring at the back of the big woman, trying to peek past her. I unbuttoned my pants and let them drop to my ankles. A moment passed.

"Your underpants, too." Her voce was quieter now but cold and strong.

I took them off slowly, but I held onto them with one hand, so they wouldn't drop to the ground. She had to bend down to look at my penis. "I thought so," she mumbled to herself, and turned around and rushed back inside the building. I quickly pulled my pants back on. The boys began to move around aimlessly. The soccer ball lay still in the middle of the yard. Then one of the boys kicked the ball against the wall, and the play resumed as if nothing had happened.

Much later, my mother told me the rest of what happened that evening when she returned from work. The landlady had summoned Mother, who realized she had to talk her way out of a bad situation. So she pretended to apologize about me, her Jewish son.

"How come you *have* a Jewish son?" the landlady inquired.

"Oh," said Mother, creating what she hoped was a rational answer, "he is an adopted child. He is not really my own. His mother asked me to take care of him, and I promised her that I would keep him safe. I would appreciate it very much if you could keep this a secret between us," my mother pleaded. The landlady was pleased that my mother was not a Jew and agreed to the secret. But my mother told me she did not trust the landlady. So, in the middle of the night, she packed a bag, and then we quietly sneaked out of the building; in the morning, we took the first train to Warsaw. My mother had heard about a bishop there who was sympathetic to Jews. She went to his church, asked to see him in his study, revealed her true identity, and pleaded for him to find a place for me in a monastery. Much later, she explained it to me. "The bishop was a very kind man. I was lucky to have met him. He found a place for you in Otwock, and he didn't ask for any money."

When I asked her why she took such a risk, she said, "I was desperate. I had no place to go and didn't know anybody. I was alone and only twenty-six years old. Where could we hide?" To me, Mother's warm eyes, small nose, and sweet mouth were so perfectly placed on her face that she looked very appealing and friendly. She wouldn't admit this to me, but I thought that since she had been pretty, spoke fluent Polish, and looked Christian, she could have easily blended into the Polish society without a Jewish-looking son by her side. I had been "unfavorable" for both of us.

In the convent, when I was in bed trying to sleep, a persistent buzz came from the darkness outside. At first, it was distracting, but when I learned that crickets were making the chirping sound, I felt soothed by them. In fact, I counted on the crickets to lull me to sleep. Every night, except when it rained, they came to keep me company and helped to take away my loneliness. On stormy nights they hid, but when the weather cleared, they always returned. Often, I had thoughts about my mother—did she find a safe place to live? Would the Germans catch her? Even the crickets could not pacify me then.

The crickets lulled me to sleep, and the birds welcomed me in the morning. Before the roosters crowed, I heard them chirping and calling each other. Hearing the birds' echoing chatter at dawn made me as happy as hearing the crickets' buzz at night. They woke me and talked to me. With time, I began to understand them and heard in their waves of chatter the news of the previous day and night. The birds gossiped about each other. Some complained that somebody ate their piece of bread; others, that a bird started a fight or other ordinary things that I myself experienced with the boys in the convent. The birds were busiest just before the sun's early light.

I learned the way of the convent of the Order of Maria's Family. Before each meal, I took my turn at blessing all the children and adults. Sometimes I was asked to make the blessing out of turn. Sister Leonia would give me the signal with a warm smile, and I would stand up and recite, "Thank you God for this daily bread, and please forgive us for our sins."

The sisters made it clear that the man I saw on the cross when I first entered the convent was Jesus, the son of God, and that all their prayers were devoted equally to him and to his father. I attended chapel every morning. In the aisle, before I went to my seat, I made the sign of the cross, saying, "In the name of the Father, and of the Son, and of the Holy Spirit. Amen."

The chapel felt like the safest and most secure place in the convent. Here, the man hung on a dark wood cross on a white wall overlooking the entire chapel. Mary, his mother, stood under him and to the right on a pedestal. I sensed in her a sweetness and kindness that were enchanting. I felt happy because I had someone to say things to, and I felt that they would listen. Jesus and his mother were always waiting for me.

Sister Leonia showed me how to darn my socks. She taught me how to make a square with the thread around the hole and then crisscross, one thread over and then under, until a cap covered the holes in my heels and toes. I could smell the soap in her habit. And when she moved closer to demonstrate how to thread the needle, her face smelled as fresh as the apples I loved to eat when the summer ended. Her hands were narrow and her fingers long, with nails cut to the edge of her fingers. I liked to be touched by them, especially when she held my hand walking across the grass back into the convent.

It was the job of the boys to work and keep the convent in good shape. One of my responsibilities was to dust the chapel daily. That was my favorite task. Another boy and I spent time by ourselves in the quiet of the space. I liked to run the cloth along the head and face of the statue of Mary. I felt the statue's eyes and nose and cheeks, imagining softness and warmth in my touch. I thought about the real Mary and pictured myself holding her hand.

The blow to my routine life came out of the blue. I was playing in back of the convent. Sister Leonia charged out of the building toward me and whispered, "The Gestapo is here." She grabbed me by my arm, and we swiftly ran into the nuns' sleeping section. She raised the cover of a bed against the wall and told me to get under it. I slid back toward the wall as far as I could, my pulse pounding in my head. The mattress was so low that I had to lie on my stomach. I turned my head toward the open end and waited. With my right ear resting on the cool wooden floor, I could feel and hear the vibrations of heavy boots becoming louder and moving closer. The thuds of Gestapo boots dazed my mind and stiffened my body. Strange voices echoed outside the room. I was afraid to move, except for my fingers: on both hands, counting one, two, three, four. The hurried beat of boots stopped by my bed. A hand lifted the bedcover and an upside-down face, framed by the white cover, riveted its blue eyes on me and commanded, "*Raus da!*" Before I could move, his arm reached in and slid me out. My head hit the bed. He dragged me behind him, pulling me on the floor, as if I were a dead animal. All the nuns and boys watched.

The two agents were about to open the front door when a voice from somewhere above me echoed, "Wait!" The Gestapo agent who held me lightened his grip around my wrist and turned to see whose voice he heard. Standing on top of the stairs and bracing himself on the railing was the tall, balding resident priest, dressed in a black soutane. His face looked pale, as if he'd been hiding from the sun. Small, round glasses were sitting on his nose and thin, white patches of hair grew above his ears. With his mellow voice, he said with authority, "Don't take him. Please, leave him here. If you arrest him, you'll have to take me, too." I heard a long silence while the Gestapo agents scrutinized the priest. Then the two Nazis looked at each other, and for reasons I still don't understand to this day, the one who had me let go of my wrist. I fell to the floor. They left without me. The sisters and boys stood frozen, watching me slowly get up.

Sister Leonia was the first to come over. She placed both hands on my head and pulled me toward her, saying, "Thank the Lord and our priest. Thank God." We walked up the stairs to the priest, and I kissed the back of his hand and repeatedly said, "Thank you, thank you, Father." On the way down, Leonia told me that she, too, was surprised that the Gestapo let me go, or didn't take both of us. Then she wanted to know how they found out about me. Who could have told them? I knew that in town, posters were hung on trees and lampposts giving rewards to anyone who found a Jew. The rewards varied; some Gestapo stations gave two kilos of sugar, others flour and some *szlotys*. I began to think too. Who gave me away? Could it have been someone I played with? I began to search for the answer in the faces of everyone in the convent, but I couldn't find a clue as to who betrayed me. I started to feel on guard, particularly when I was changing clothes or going to the bathroom. From that time on, the only place I felt safe was in the chapel, where Mary and her son waited for me.

One day, as I was searching for Sister Leonia, I came into a room that looked as if it were a private study for the nuns. Curious, I entered the room. The walls were lined with books. On one side, set against a brick wall, was a sculpture made of bronze. A man stood on one leg, tilted to one side on a large ball. The other leg was extended out, parallel to the ground. One arm pointed down, the other up. He looked as if he were going to tip over and fall. His mouth was open and his face looked frightened. Yet he was kept in balance by a bird that sat on top of the foot that was extended in the air.

"Strange how a little bird keeps that man from falling off the world, isn't it?" an unfamiliar voice said, taking me by surprise.

Mother Superior, Sister Gertruda, gave me a short lecture about birds: they pair up and stay loyal to each other for a long time, she said, and they usually travel in pairs. They are very social, especially the small ones. In Poland, Sister Gertruda said, "we have birds called herons that soar and glide with big wings—finches, strong birds with a black head and rusty-colored full body and white paint below their eyes, and they sing duets and travel in pairs. Ever see a wood pigeon—dark hair with a proud beak?"

I shook my head.

* * *

In the beginning, I recited the prayers and practiced the rituals in motoric repetition, like a parrot. With time, the prayers and other practices became natural and intimate, making me feel that I belonged and that I had a place in a community where I was safe.

I learned that by making the sign of the cross of Jesus, I could make my prayers stronger and my wishes come true. At night, before I went to bed, I, like most other boys, knelt by my bed and prayed with my eyes closed. I didn't pray solely to Jesus, as I was taught, but directly to God. The God to whom I prayed was indeed almighty, but I felt that he had a special and personal watch over me. This private relationship was a secret I kept from everyone, including Sister Leonia.

"Oh, God, thank you for taking care of me. Thank you. Please listen to me. Please make sure my mother visits me Sunday. Please protect her. I will pray in the chapel every day and at every meal. And don't let them find me. Please. I will be good." I crossed myself slowly from right to left, the same way the nuns did.

During the first year, my mother kept her promise and came most Sundays. She brought rare and precious gifts. Once she brought a hard-boiled egg. Out on the grass, she carefully peeled it while two friends and I watched. I divided the egg into three parts, and we slowly ate our slice. Another time, she brought a large, red apple. I divided that into three parts and shared it. And one time, she brought a raw egg just for me.

She punctured the top with a key and carved a hole. She told me to drink it. I hesitated, but she said I needed it because I had little to eat. I made a sour face, but I put my mouth to the opened egg, tilted my head back, and let the silky egg roll past my tongue as fast as I could.

After that visit from Mother, my daily prayers in the morning, noon, and night continued over weeks and months but failed to summon my mother on Sunday, or any other day. Almost a year passed without seeing her. The memory of her voice promising Sunday visits moved further and further away and began to fade. I came to be resigned to her permanent absence. My mother's image was transformed into a muted ghost standing alongside the fading images of my father, uncle, and grandparents.

Since the first day at the convent, I was instructed that the best way to go to sleep was to lie on my back with my right hand folded over my heart and left hand on my stomach. I felt fine feeling my heart, but I couldn't understand why they would want me to feel my empty and hungry stomach. Nevertheless, it was a ritual I followed nightly as I waited for the sound of crickets.

One night I awoke and tiptoed to the bathroom to pee. I was always frightened I'd be found out, so I peed into the toilet and not the urinal, even when no one was around. When I returned, I heard one boy moan and another talk angrily in his sleep. While they were dreaming, the boy next to my bed cried and whimpered until he tired and fell back to sleep. It was almost dawn. I lay with my eyes closed, eagerly waiting for my friends, the birds, to greet me. But this particular morning they were late sleepers. Although the sun was still far away, some of its light began to appear. I wondered why they slept so late.

I decided to go out and check what was happening. I sneaked out of the convent's side door, walked past the grass, and climbed over the wall that lined the grounds. The light was dimmed, so I had to strain my eyes to see. Across the road sat two black birds high on a limb. They watched and waited. Two other birds flew from left to right.

The sun's early light shone on the white hair and light shirt worn by a man who limped slowly along the dirt road. He moved his right leg first, then dragged his left so that it was even with his right. He repeated the motion as he made his way forward. I watched him with curiosity: why was this man wounded? I heard no shots or explosions. The sky was low that morning, with round, dark-silver clouds moving across in the same direction as the man walking.

I walked quietly and cautiously. I noticed a big, dark bird sitting on a bare branch of a tree. He was perched upright, tail down, head up. I slowed down and then stopped, not wanting to scare the bird. The bird's beak and eyes were pointed directly at me. I stiffened and focused on the bird. The sun began to show more of its light. To my surprise, the bird jumped off the branch and glided down to a spot about ten feet in front of me. I now stood particularly still, fearful that the bird would fly away. A strange thing happened. Rather than fly off, scared, the bird actually turned around three times and faced me again, his big beak pointed right at me. I stared at the bird in amazement. We both stood in silence, staring at each other. Nothing happened. A few quiet moments passed. Then the bird again swung around several times and faced me. This time I noticed that the end of the bird's tail was frayed and covered with blotches of light gray. The tail looked like it had been charred!

As soon as I recognized what had happened to the bird, it flew off and disappeared into the woods. How did he burn himself? I thought. And why was it so important to the bird that I see the burn?

I returned to the convent and my bed as quietly as I had left, feeling very puzzled. I slipped under the covers, closed my eyes, and waited for the chatter to begin. When dawn fully arrived, the birds woke up. I heard one bird in particular calling to the others in a sharp, raspy voice. By the loudness of the sound, I assumed it was the big bird I had met earlier in the morning. Other birds responded to the voice.

"Don't tell him. Why make him more worried? He already knows his father died," one voice cautioned.

"And his grandmother, he knows that, too?" added another.

"He only knows that they were captured and sent by train to a prison camp and then disappeared. Maybe they are not dead. He is not sure," a new voice spoke up.

Their voices softened to make it hard for me to hear. But I heard them anyway.

The big voice, which I was sure belonged to the bird with the burned tail, spoke. He had flown to Warsaw, so he could report back to them about what was happening. He said: "I saw Warsaw burning, full of smoke. The Russians were bombing the Germans. And the Germans and Poles were running away from the fighting. In the crowd, I saw his mother. He should know."

"His mother—you saw his mother?" an excited voice asked.

"Yes. She is alive. But she was moving away from Warsaw with the rest of the people. That's how I got my tail burned—I flew too close to the flames to find her."

"But you did see his mother!"

"Yes, I told you. She was running away from the smoke and fire in the other direction, away from us. She couldn't come this way."

"Why not?" the bird wanted to know.

"Because there was too much fighting and bombing by the Russians. She would have been killed if she tried."

"We should tell him. It's been a whole year since he heard from his mother!"

The last voice I heard warned the others to be cautious about telling me. "If he hears that Warsaw is burning, he'll think his mother and uncle might die, too."

A long silence followed this chatter. One bird called repeatedly over and over again, but nobody answered. I heard the silence, and I became frightened.

"She... is... alive?" I whispered to myself and noticed my forefinger sliding along my thumb.

* * *

A few months later, on a Sunday after chapel, the sisters rushed all of us to the basement, saying that the fighting between the Russians and Germans was getting too close to the convent. The basement was divided into several sections that looked like stalls with concrete walls. The floor was actually bare earth that was covered with hay. In one corner lay a couple rolls of hay. Five boys were assigned to a cubicle. The window in my cubicle had been barricaded with brick and stone that made my space dark. During this particular week, we were confined to the convent. But when any shooting or explosion was heard, the nuns immediately shouted for us to go below. I felt as if all of us flew over the wooden basement stairs, landing on the ground with the hay softening our fall. Sometimes we spent most of the day below before we were given the clear signal to come up. On occasion, when I was tired or bored, I slept on the floor, piling up a bunch of hay to make a pillow. The air and straw smelled damp, but I liked the feeling of sinking into the deep layers of hay.

That week, in 1944, when trees lost their leaves and exposed their barren branches, my convent was liberated by an explosion. The *boom* I heard outside my basement window slammed me against the opposite wall. Red and orange blotches flashed in my eyes, and smoke, together with strange smells from the explosion, filled my cubicle. The window that had been barricaded was punctured, and the opening allowed light to enter on foggy rays that angled downward. Above me, I heard the nuns' loud voices.

"The Russians think that we are German soldiers in hiding," cried one nun.

"We have to show them who we are!" another said.

"I will go outside," a voice announced.

"All right, but take a white towel," the first voice yelled.

From the basement, still stunned and pinned to the wall, I imagined Sister Leonia in her dark habit and white cornette, walking outside, waving the white towel over her head. She must have calmed the Russians because there were no more explosions. Instead, Russian soldiers with bayonets fixed to their rifles stormed into the basement searching for Germans. They thrust their bayonets into piles of hay where they suspected Germans were hiding. I tried to push myself into the concrete wall to escape the long, shiny blades that pointed at everything and everyone. The blades, with their green-uniformed soldiers, moved silently and swiftly through the basement. I only heard their sound, the slicing of hay and grinding crackle as they hit rocks embedded in the ground. Now and then, I heard a soldier utter something I couldn't understand. The other boys in my stall were silent, their wide-open eyes watching the blades as the soldiers moved through our cubicle.

When the Russians left, finding no Germans, Mother Superior called us upstairs and announced, "The war is over, children. We have all been freed!" And she led us in a prayer to the Lord in gratitude for our liberation.

Following Mother Superior's thankful prayers and the realization that the war had finally come to an end for us, a new emotion gripped me. While I had experienced the terror of the Gestapo and loneliness throughout the war, the agony of waiting to know whether my mother had survived was the most painful. I waited for her to pick me up every day for many months. If she had been killed, would my uncle, as she promised that first day at the convent, come for me? I had to wait for him, too. Was he alive? I waited and waited.

Every knock on the front door made me run toward the lobby. I wasn't the only one. All the boys who had parents at the beginning of the war ran toward the door. A knock or a commotion at the front door produced a wave of boys coming out of the chapel, dormitory, or classroom.

With each knock, only one boy was made happy. The rest of us returned, with our heads down, to what we were doing.

For a long time, I ran for each knock on the door. But as my disappointment mounted, I began to walk toward the knock. Then I stopped walking, and I just listened for her voice. I often thought, Will I spend the rest of my life here with the nuns and orphaned boys?

I was in my dormitory when I heard a voice in the distance, a voice so familiar and comforting that I felt as if my body were immersed in a pool of warm water. My mother's voice revived in me the spirit of peace and happiness I had experienced with her before the war. It came over me like a flash, and it dissipated just as quickly as my mind returned to the present. The voice came closer and closer until I saw my mother standing at the edge of the dormitory. I felt my eyes swell, and I walked slowly toward her. I didn't run, as I had seen other, older boys do toward their parents. My mother rushed toward me and embraced me, holding my head with both hands. My mind felt far away. Sister Leonia stood nearby, smiling. I saw tears in her eyes for the first time.

That afternoon, I said goodbye to the boys who were still waiting. I felt very bad for them, for they still didn't know the fate of their parents. I said goodbye to all the nuns and kissed the priest's hand for the second time. My mother thanked the nuns profusely and promised to stay in contact and to help them. Before we left, Sister Leonia asked if she could see me alone. She took my hand and led me to the chapel.

As always, Mary and her son on the wall waited inside. Sister Leonia knelt and prayed out loud, thanking the Lord for my mother's arrival and blessing me to have a good life. Her eyes watered again. I, too, knelt and prayed. Deep sadness overcame me. I didn't want to leave.

Sister Leonia stood up, wiped her eyes with a handkerchief she pulled from inside her sleeve, took my hand, and led me out of the chapel. She asked me if I would visit her sometime. "Yes, yes," I replied, not knowing where I was going or where I would live.

It was late afternoon when mother and I walked out the door of the convent. I stopped on the walkway and listened for the birds. Only a few voices chattered, but I still couldn't understand them. I felt mad that the birds had stopped talking to me or about me. A pair of dark birds flew by and perched themselves on a branch. We gazed at each other in silence, and I felt like throwing stones at them. My mother looked puzzled. Then she took my hand, and we left.

Note: The Otwock convent cared for orphaned and homeless Christian children or for children whose parents placed them there for safety for the duration of the war. Starting in 1942, it also provided sanctuary for a limited number of Jewish refugee children. In Poland, there were about 190 such convents, organized in independent orders and communities, each with its own habits, traditions, and goals. Some asked for money, about 8 thousand *zlotys* per year, in advance, for each child. At the end of the war, those convents wanting money would not release the children until the parents paid them. Maria's Family did not ask my mother for any remuneration. Regardless of the financial policy, the nuns and priests who resided in these convents risked their lives by hiding Jewish children. The mortal risk to the sisters for protecting a Jew transcended their vows.

The Early Adventures of an Immigrant in America

On a warm spring evening in Munich, Mother returned from work to our apartment, practically bursting with something she had to tell me. "I have a surprise for you. Guess what it is!"

"A new soccer ball?"

"No! Guess again. It's something big. Something we've been waiting for," she said, lifting her arms in the air.

"A new bicycle! Yes?"

She came closer to me, leaned over, placed her hands on my shoulder, and blurted, "We are going to America! I got the visa today!"

Because visas to America were limited for Jews, my mother and I had waited three years to go to America. After the war hurricanes in Europe, we, like most other refugees from Eastern Europe, migrated to Munich as a temporary place before choosing resettlement in a new country. Mother had a choice of going to Australia ("No, too far, and we don't know anybody there"), South America (same reason), Israel ("I want peace—I've had enough of war"), and America ("That's where we want to go. We have cousins there, and it's a good place for us.")

While waiting for the visa in Munich, we lived in a well-lit, one-room apartment in a small building near the Isar

River. The apartment was on the ground floor, and the window about five feet off the ground. My friend and I would make slingshots from rubber bands and shoot at pigeons from that window. What was even more fun was when we'd throw pennies on the street by the window and wait for ladies who were looking for coins. We crumbled small pieces of paper and dipped them in black ink. When they arrived and bent to pick up our bait, we threw the wet, inky paper balls so they struck them in the back of the neck, and then we quickly crouched below the window, listening to their grunts and curses.

Mother enrolled me in a Hebrew school. It was not religious, but everything taught or spoken in that school was in Hebrew. As soon as you stepped in the door, you were required to speak Hebrew, which seemed as tough to me as Arabic or English. But within a few months, I understood geography, mathematics, and history in Hebrew.

Inside the school, we danced the *hora* in a big circle to the music a teacher played on the accordion, and some talented kids sang Israeli folk songs. I felt safe and warm there. All the children felt familiar, even if I didn't know them. We were instant brothers and sisters. At the end of the class day, I happily played soccer in the schoolyard. We quickly choose sides and made goalposts out of our books. I was excited to run, argue about fouls, yell, and sometimes even score a goal. I felt unselfconscious and free for the first time in my life

Polish is the language I was born into and spoke most of my childhood. Because I lived in Germany, I had to learn German, which I did by talking to other people and from my mother, who had learned it during the war. The classes in school were mixed in ages, as there weren't enough teachers or students. In my class, most kids were older than me. There were more girls than boys because girls survived the war at twice the rate of boys, whose circumcision betrayed them. I, like the others, was simply happy to be alive and away from the terror. I felt relieved that the outside danger was gone, at least for now. I'm sure none of us were aware of the internal wounds and pain the war had caused until much later, if at all. While all our experiences were similar, we never talked about them. Everybody took part in building a wall of silence around the Holocaust. We behaved as if life naturally restarted in 1945 and the war was simply an interruption, a bump in the road.

* * *

I had forgotten about the visa and America. Mother's disappointment at my lack of enthusiasm was plain to see. I felt bad that I didn't feel as good as she did. I was happy at Hebrew school and didn't want to leave my friends behind.

We took an American troop transport ship from Bremer-Haven, Germany, to New York City and arrived on May 18, 1949. I was eleven years old. During the stormy, two-week voyage, I, unlike most of the other passengers, did not throw up. My mother, who slept in a different part of the ship with the other women and girls, also did not get sick. I think we were the only two lucky ones out of more than a hundred. My only mishap occurred in the middle of the night, when I forgot I was at the top of a triple bunk bed and stepped off to go to the bathroom. No one woke up.

My first night in America was spent at the Hebrew Immigrant Aid Society's (HIAS) immigration center on Lafayette Street in Manhattan, now the site of Joe Papp's Public Theater. The new arrivals were separated and put into two large halls furnished with army cots lined up in several rows. One hall was for women and girls, and the other, men and boys. Before we parted for the night, Mother gave me a hug and stroked my forehead, pressing my hair to the side.

"You're a good boy," she said softly, so no one could hear.

I felt sad to separate from her during the night and sleep with strangers. But then, I was used to it. Being alone became as ordinary as being together with Mother. Some adults smiled at me, but the children kept to themselves, as did I. The cots were similar to those on the ship, except that they were all single beds, so I didn't have to worry about falling. We slept and ate there for two weeks, the maximum stay allowed. Then we were on our own.

During our time at the immigration center, mother looked for a job and an apartment with the help of HIAS. She found a room on the Lower East Side of Manhattan in the shadow of the El train. It was a walk-up on the third floor, hot and much darker than our sunny room in Munich. I wondered where the money tree was.

I had to get used to the rattle of trains passing our only window. The rattle got into my body, so it felt like the apartment was in continuous chatter. Luckily, there were fewer trains at night. I was amazed by the magic of how this railroad floated in the air, held up by skinny steel posts. As I watched them pass, I was mesmerized by the cars' rhythmic blocking of the sun. The light in between cars blinked, like eyelids, on/off, on/off, until they all passed and let the sky open up once again. The cars flew by my window with a steady beat: left, right, left, right. The sound of wheels on tracks echoed a song that said: life-goes-on, life-goes-on. It reminded me of the soothing lullabies crickets and birds sang to me in the convent in Poland. I welcomed the noisy music. Quiet solitude disturbed me and made me restless.

Mother found employment in a sweatshop working at a sewing machine. The job made no use of her formal education, but at least it was a job. Before the war, she had lived in the house her father built. She went to dental school in France for one year. It was an amazing accomplishment for a woman, and for a Jew. She then returned to Poland to marry my father and give birth me. Two years later, the war broke out. I felt bad for her, now sweating in a hot, crowded room with other immigrants.

I was placed in sixth grade for six weeks. I spoke pidgin English. The teacher tried to help me make friends and introduced me to another boy who had just arrived from Europe. I think she thought everyone from Europe spoke the same language. Stanley was my height, with wavy, dark hair combed straight back. He had large eyes, a wide nose, and long eyelashes. He was thin like me. I tried to speak to him in my broken English, but I got no response, only a puzzled look. I tried Polish. Nothing. Then German and Hebrew. Still no response. All I got were raised shoulders and words I didn't understand. Turned out he was Bulgarian and only spoke Bulgarian. I was able to communicate better with American kids than with him.

But in our dogged effort to communicate with each other, Stanley and I became best friends. Neither of us spoke about our past, nor asked each other questions about what had happened to us. I was locked in. So was he. Stanley lived with his father. At first, I was curious to know what it was like to live with a father, and I felt jealous. I had the urge to spend more time in his apartment to get familiar with his father. I never knew where his mother was. But his father was never home, and Stanley had an independent life with no one to report to. He never talked about it, but I felt bad for him, because he really was alone. My mother often asked me to invite him for supper, which he accepted. It was comforting to have another boy in my apartment.

One day, a distant American cousin invited us to dinner. They lived in Westchester and owned a men's clothing store in Manhattan. I don't recall what the cousins looked like, because that was the first and only time I saw them. Everybody hugged, as if we were close. Mother seemed happy to meet them. My cousin looked at me, and she said to Mother, "Oh, he is a handsome boy, but he is too skinny." I was dizzy with the aromas of meats and sweets, which made me even hungrier. OK, I thought, then let's eat.

To my disappointment, we got the house tour before we got the food. It was a huge house—two stories, with at least two bathrooms, a few bedrooms, a separate place to eat, and a parlor to sit in. I stopped counting the rooms. The whole house was theirs. I was amazed. I was afraid I'd get lost if I wandered off into the bathroom. I felt small and poor.

Before supper, the three cousins sat around talking excitedly, like dogs on the street barking at each other. I wandered around and noticed on the kitchen counter the largest bowl of strawberries I had ever seen. I reached for one and was about to taste it, when the woman cousin rushed over, pointed a finger at me, and said in English, "Don't eat that!"

I backed off. Mother rushed toward us and placed her hand on the back of my head. Her eyes widened and mouth narrowed. With a put-on smile, she looked up at her taller cousin and said in Polish, "Oh, he was just looking. He had never seen so many big strawberries before."

We had a feast like none I had ever enjoyed. We ate brisket, roasted chicken, carrots, string beans, warmed bread with butter, and salad with tomatoes. For dessert, we had apple kugel with cinnamon, part of the aroma I had smelled. I tried to eat slowly and not look too eager. When the white bowl of strawberries finally came, my mother got the first choice. She moved the bowl toward me, and with a large spoon scooped a big bunch of shiny berries onto my white plate. The fruit was juicy and tasty, and I would have eaten all of it if allowed. I hid my pleasure.

When they were drinking coffee, the cousin asked me questions about myself. I told them that I had just got a job after school delivering clothes from a dry cleaner. "I made four dollars in tips on the weekend," I said proudly. Mother kicked me under the table. I realized she didn't want me to tell anybody about how much I made—as if I were making buckets of dollars. She liked to keep things secret.

Next day, I heard Mother talking in Polish to a friend on the phone about this cousin, "Yes, she said to him, 'Don't take the strawberries.' Why would she say no to him? Doesn't she know where he comes from? She shouldn't have done that."

One day in June, after only one month in America, my mother told me, "I found a place for you to go in the summer. It's in the country, with fresh air and other boys and girls. You will have fun, and they will take good care of you and give you good food. It's called summer camp. Don't worry, I will visit you. It's only for two months. All right?"

She kissed me on the forehead and waited for me to agree. I had no idea what she was talking about. And the word "camp" was not a happy-sounding word to me, but I trusted her. Within a few days, I was on a bus with other children on the way to this "camp."

The best thing Mother did for me in America was to send me to this summer camp in New Jersey. We had no money, so she got support from a Jewish organization. I was forced to speak English, because no one spoke anything else. And by the end of camp, two months later, not only had I learned enough English to have a conversation, but I also learned to play American sports like softball and basketball, previously unknown to me.

The kids and counselors were all friendly. Many went out of their way to be nice, since I was a survivor from the war. Most of the counselors and kids were Jewish, so I didn't have to hide or pretend otherwise. Sleeping in a bunk with fourteen other kids my age left me feeling safer than I'd felt in a long time. When peeing at the urinal, I noticed that other boys were also circumcised. I didn't have to hide. I was no longer different.

The cabin had lightbulbs hanging from a wire. I could hardly read with the light they emitted, so I borrowed a flashlight. I used it under the covers after "lights out" to read my favorite book in German, which I had brought from Munich: *Der Ruf der Wildnis (The Call of the Wild)* by Jack London. I felt self-conscious reading a German book.

The cots were arranged evenly in rows against the wall, much like the cots in the convent where I had stayed during the war. I had to make my own bed the way my counselor showed us. It had to be clean and crisp. The green blanket, tightly folded with hospital corners, dared the inspecting counselor to bounce a coin on it. My clothes had to be stored in my locker and shoes neatly placed under the bed. I liked the bunk's cleanliness and order. Some kids hated these routines, but they actually made me feel safe.

After inspection, we had breakfast in the dining hall, which turned into a social hall after dinner. We sat at assigned picnic tables. I liked the food, though some others complained all the time. I devoured eggs, Wheaties or hot cereal, bread, and as much milk as I wanted. Lunches and dinners were also big. You could even get seconds. I was thrilled.

The camp had sports I'd never heard of—softball, basketball, badminton. I only knew soccer. Counselors and other campers explained the games to me. In softball, I first played the outfield, where they put all the weak players. Later on, I played third base, which I liked better because I got more balls and could show off my strong arm throwing to first.

Camp was a joyous wonderland where no one asked me about the details of my inner life.

Sometimes, at lunches and dinners, kids at one table would begin a song that spread to the entire dining hall. All the boys and girls would join in spontaneously, and you could hear a chorus echoing the song. One afternoon, I walked closely alongside a pretty girl who smiled at me. She liked me! At dinner, all the kids in the hall began to sing,

"Linda and Clem, sitting in a tree, K-I-S-S-I-N-G.

First comes love, then comes marriage,

Then comes Linda with a baby carriage."

Halfway through, I realized they were singing about me! I turned red, and my body stiffened. I was so embarrassed that I pretended I didn't like it. But inside, I felt famous. Everybody seemed to know my name—even if I had no idea what the song meant.

Camp life was open, playful, and free—the opposite of hiding and pretending to be somebody else. My spirits quickly rose. At night, in the social hall, campers sang folk songs I did not know, but I felt warmth from the melodies and a wonderful, exhilarating sense of belonging, an experience that was totally new to me. I heard the tunes and watched the happy faces and rhythmic body movements of boys and girls bouncing and swaying together. The music was earthy and upbeat, touching me deeply, like an ancient tribal chant.

Sometimes at these moments, I got teary listening to happy songs. I imagined that camp was what heaven was like, and my past was what hell was like. I must have done something right to be here. God was looking out for me. I was as grateful to my mother for sending me to camp as I was for her saving my life during the war.

When camp ended, I was very sad. On the last day, we all got into buses and sang songs. I didn't know them, but I did my best to sing along. Some kids were happy to return to their homes and friends in their neighborhood. Others, like me, were sad, and most probably felt a little of both. I was returning to a one-room apartment in a strange city in a foreign country. When we got off the bus back in New York and said goodbye, some kids hugged me and promised to stay in touch. As we all went our separate ways, I couldn't shake my sadness. I had lost my wonderland.

There, among the other parents, was my mother to greet me, with a big smile and wet eyes. I felt bad for feeling sad. I ran to her, and she took me in her arms. I hugged her back. I didn't tell her I was already missing camp. When she embraced me, I felt her love, relieved that she was there. And just when I felt calmed by her arms around me, my mind slipped into a fear of never seeing her again and being stranded, completely alone. I was glad that in camp no one had asked me about my war experiences. It was a relief to forget, if only briefly.

While I was at camp, Mother had moved us to the Upper West Side, into a one-room studio above Stark's restaurant on Broadway and 90th Street. I was glad to be away from that subway-rattled apartment by the El. It was a simple move since we only had enough things to fill two suitcases. My new home had lots of light because it was on the corner, with windows on both sides. It was cheery and clean, and the only noise came from Broadway traffic.

That year, I was moved one class forward into a "progressive" junior high school near my home. Stanley, my first real friend in this new country, was there, too. Every morning, the principal transmitted her message through speakers in every classroom. She would say, "Good morning, everyone. This is Dr. Sweeting speaking. Please pay attention to the following announcements and schedule changes…" and then she would announce teacher substitutes or special events or changes in lunch times. We all thought this was funny and weird, but I felt reassured by the regularity of the talks and daily welcoming remarks.

One boy in my class, Ernie, was first-generation Italian. He wore black glasses that matched his thick, black hair, which he parted on the left side. He was about my height but chunkier, and he had a sarcastic sense of humor that I found smart and funny. I didn't speak much to him until all boys were required to choose two out of three home economics courses: cleaning, cooking, or sewing. This was what they called "progressive." Since I already did the cleaning at home and felt I had nothing to learn and didn't want to do it again in school, I chose cooking and sewing. Ernie picked the same courses, where we cooked and sewed together. Cooking was easy. We had a kitchen in the school, and for breakfast, I volunteered to make the simplest item—cocoa.

Sewing was more difficult. We had to make a piece of clothing. I went to Woolworth's to buy a pattern for a short-sleeved shirt. I bought yellow cotton fabric. In class, I laid out the material, placed the paper pattern over it, and cut the fabric along its edge. Then I sewed the pieces together after waiting my turn for one of the sewing machines to be free and for the teacher to show me how to use it. I got mixed up and sewed the collar on the bottom of the shirt. The teacher let me undo it and correct it so I could pass. Ernie laughed at me and made me feel all right.

After school, I loved going to Ernie's apartment, which smelled of garlic and tomatoes. Ernie's mother cooked delicious lasagna, over which she sprinkled freshly grated Parmesan cheese; with it she served warm Italian bread with butter. We ate cannoli for dessert. The tastes and smells were all new to me and different from my mother's Eastern European cooking. Still, my mother's chicken noodle soup, into which she sprinkled lots of dill, remains my most memorable and soothing food. To this day, when I smell dill, I feel her presence.

Ernie's mother, who came to New York from Italy as a young girl, had a calm presence, and always greeted me with an inviting smile. She owned a flower shop, where I earned money delivering flowers on busy weekends and holidays. I remember the thrill of the first tip I got. It was a quarter. I jumped in the air to celebrate. I thought this was the beginning of making lots of money for myself.

Ernie and I spent a lot of time in each other's homes, but because I loved his mother's cooking, I probably ate more at his house than he ate at mine. Once, during lunch, we walked into the schoolyard, and without a thought, I put my arm around his shoulder. This was a natural thing for two friends to do where I came from, but here, some of the guys made fun of us, calling us "fags." I was embarrassed and was afraid to touch Ernie again.

My friends and I went to the same high school on the West Side, in midtown Manhattan. Bruce was the smartest, and more widely read than any of us. He wore round glasses that he habitually pushed up his nose when he was thinking hard about a problem. He did not look strong and was no athlete. Yet he gained respect because of his smarts, fearless attitude, and status as "most valuable member" of the visual aid squad that showed movies and slides. In English class, while I struggled with vocabulary assignments, having to look up most of the words in the dictionary, Bruce just knew the definitions without studying. It was as if he had taken the course several times over. In some of the classes, he was bored and would sit in the back reading *The New York Times*. He read it the right way, too. He would fold the pages vertically in half and read each quarter. He read it openly, as if challenging the teacher. As expected, there were many arguments between the teacher and him. Sometimes being his friend was embarrassing, but I looked up to him and valued his advice.

In class, during an exercise, I would lean over and ask, "What does *fastidious* mean?"

He'd whisper back, "Meticulous, or hard to please."

High school was tough. Most students were commercial majors, having no intention of going to college. Whites were a small minority, Jews even smaller. Fighting was a common thing, especially among Puerto Rican and black gangs. Most troubling for me was witnessing big kids picking on smaller kids, bilking them of their money or lunch. I was too scared to help.

I learned to get through high school without a fight by walking the middle line between being a fighter and chicken. If you looked tough, like you were itching for a fight, you'd get a fight. But even if you beat the other guy, he'd come back the next day with a few buddies and take care of you. A Puerto Rican friend—tall, muscular, and tough looking—was picked on by another kid for no reason. I think he wanted to make a name for himself.

"Don't mess with me. You'll get hurt!" my friend warned him.

But he wouldn't stop and threw a punch. My friend then knocked him to the ground with one strike. The kid got up and fled. Next day, after school, this kid came back with three friends. One of them knifed my friend in the back, damaging his shoulder.

I was thin and didn't look tough. So, I walked the hallways with a determined gait, chest out, pretending to be strong but not looking for a fight. But I decided I needed protection or respect. So, I joined the swimming team. It was the worst team in the city, but I didn't care. I got to wear the athlete's jacket with a big *C* symbolizing my school. I looked like a jock and automatically got respect. I could tell by the way the big guys looked at me walking down the hallway. They first beamed their eyes on the letter on my jacket, then at my eyes, and walked on.

I swam the breaststroke in the one hundred yards and in relay races. We practiced in a pool that required us to swim naked. A "sanitary thing," we were told. (How does a bathing suit make our bodies more dirty?) The coach made us practice diving, which we did naked, with our organs hanging. That is scary and painful if you don't land right. Some of us dove with only one arm out, the other holding ourselves so as not to get slammed.

At graduation, the entire auditorium was full, including the balcony. We must have had over 400 graduates, all throwing their caps in the air when the ceremony was over. Bruce, Ernie, and I hung out at various bars looking for something special to do to celebrate. We met Christopher, another graduate. He was the only one I knew whose parents had a car. Miraculously, he talked his dad into lending him his brandnew, four-door Ford for the night.

We headed for the Catskills, where his parents had a cabin. His father, a devout Catholic, made him swear he wouldn't drink and drive. Before we left, we chipped in for a bottle of Johnnie Walker. We didn't drink until we got to the cabin after midnight. It was a small, dusty, one-bedroom cabin. We searched the cabinets, and all we could find were cans of beans and corn, which we devoured with our Scotch. We didn't even bother with dishes; we each got forks and passed the cans around.

Before the sun began its rise, we decided to drive to the little lake nearby to swim. Since none of us had expected to go swimming, we had not packed bathing suits. We drove to the lake that early so we could swim naked. We were looped, and I was glad I wasn't driving. (I didn't have a license, anyway.) At the lake, still drinking from the same bottle, we cooled off in the water. All of us swam to a little island across from the beach. Ernie left his glasses behind on the beach. We decided to play a joke on him. We dove into the water and raced toward the beach, leaving Ernie alone. At the beach, we yelled, "Bye, bye Ernie. We're going home!" The sun began to rise.

We were laughing so hard I cried. We ran naked to the car, fighting for the only towel to dry ourselves. We took off for a short ride, just enough to scare Ernie. Christopher drove along a gravel road that was about to be covered with blacktop; as we drove we left a trail of dust swirling behind us. We weren't going fast, but Christopher was having fun swaying the car left and right. I could hear the stones hitting the car under my feet, and I was sober enough to get nervous. Then the car slid down a hill at an angle and hit a rock that flipped us all upside down, and then it swirled 180 degrees. For a few seconds, it felt like I was in a roller-coaster ride at Coney Island. My heart pounded. The car landed on its roof, about face, engine smoking. When the car stopped moving, I had a momentary terror that one of us was dead. I saw the headlines: "Boy dies in car accident. All occupants naked."

"What the fuck happened? Is everybody OK?" I blurted out in a daze. Sitting in the back seat, I waited to see if I had any pain or breaks in my body. I felt nothing, except the hammering in my chest. I struggled to climb out the window. Christopher did the same, but Bruce was in the passenger seat, not moving. I looked at him, lying upside down on his head and shoulders, his legs above him.

"Bruce, you OK?" For a moment, I thought he was dead.

"Ugh," he grunted, trying to stroke his head. I pulled his door open and helped him out. He staggered out slowly.

The engine was smoking. We panicked and ran for cover on the side of the road, waiting for the car to explode. Nothing happened. Only steam rose from the busted radiator. The sun was now fully out, and my heart wouldn't stop pounding. We were totally naked, and far more sober than before.

"We have to get back to the beach and get our clothes!" someone said.

"And get Ernie," I said.

I tried to run, but my bare feet hurt on the gravel. I got down the hill, touching the stones as little as possible, holding myself in case a car came by. You could hear a chorus of "shit, "damn," and "Jesus" from all of us. I feared a car would go by and report us for indecent exposure. Fear and embarrassment pushed me faster toward my clothes.

At the beach, I saw Ernie, who had swum back from the island and was now collecting flowers. When we told him what had happened, he just smiled and went on gathering daisies. We dressed quickly, pushing Ernie to feel our urgency. I was relieved to walk with my shoes on along a familiar gravel road.

Christopher made a call from a phone booth, and we met the police at the upside-down Ford, which looked like a dead cockroach on its back. The officer asked the driver to tell him what happened. Chris was nervous, stuttering to explain how he got the car into this position. Trying to help, I interrupted, careful not to breathe too close to the officer. I said that the road was slippery because it was not paved... and wasn't the county responsible? The officer asked whether we wanted a ticket for drunk driving, too. That shut us all up.

We returned to New York by train. I couldn't imagine what horror Christopher was feeling, having to face his father. They weren't rich. He was too nervous to go home alone, so Bruce and I agreed to tail along to offer support and forestall a beating. The father opened the door; he must have sensed something was wrong because he didn't invite us in. I was grateful.

After high school, we all went our separate ways to different colleges and careers. I knew I wanted to be a professional, but I didn't know what profession to study. Driving me was my desire to do something that would make me independent of mother's financial support. I was pushed toward medicine by my mother and my uncle, who was a doctor. They felt I was smart and could get through medical school with little problem. But I was lost and confused, without real direction. In my confusion, and with my family's urging, I agreed to go into medicine. I got a scholarship to Yeshiva University, in premed.

The first day of school, in the lobby, a man came out of one of the offices, pointed at me, and waved his hand for me to come to him. I entered his office. He sat down behind his desk and said, "You are not wearing a yarmulke."

"Oh, I am sorry; I didn't know I was supposed to."

"Yes, everybody here does." He reached into his drawer and gave me a folded black cap. I opened it, put it on my head, and went to my first class. I was not brought up religious or Orthodox. I never wore a yarmulke outside of a synagogue.

The next day, in front of the main building, I put on my yarmulke. I walked into the lobby and found the same man standing outside his office, looking at me.

I went toward him, and he pointed to my head.

"I am wearing a yarmulke," I said defensively.

"Yes, but I saw you put it on outside. You're supposed to wear it all the time."

"You mean everywhere? In the subway? Even when I play basketball?"

"Yes. All the time," he declared.

I went to the morning classes. Even though we were all Jewish, I felt awkward and different from the other boys. They had gone to yeshivas, whereas I attended an integrated public school. They were religious; I was not. Still, I felt a kinship because they were Jewish, and so I tried to feel that I belonged.

Standing by the urinals, every boy I saw peeing next to me had his foreskin pushed back. The same as me. That felt comforting. The embarrassment and fear that I had felt in Poland that came from being different and Jewish faded in this bathroom.

At lunch, a few boys invited me to join them. We went to a local kosher deli.

Thoughtlessly, or perhaps not, I ordered a ham and cheese sandwich on rye, a favorite of mine. Before I realized my error, they all burst out laughing, thinking I was making a joke. I laughed along, pretending to be funny.

After lunch, the boys returned to school, but I walked past the entrance and into the nearest subway station, running down the stairs to take the train home. I decided Yeshiva wasn't for me. I then enrolled in City College, which was free. I chose engineering, because I could get a job right after college and make lots of money. My choice was my own. I imagined when I graduated college I could rent my own apartment on West End Avenue, rescue Mother from the sweatshop, eat at expensive restaurants, and even buy a car!

The Bell

I awoke to the sound of the ringing bell. Startled, I rushed to my mother's room. It was 3:30 in the morning. A few weeks earlier, I had given her a blue ceramic bell to ring in case I couldn't hear her call me.

"I have to get up," she said softly. With only the moon illuminating her bed, my mother reached out toward me with both arms, which cast a faint and uneven shadow on the blanket. Her eyes searched for me in the dim light. When she finally focused on me, I could sense in her face her self-conscious plea: "Please, help me." I thought, how many times had my children, when they were young, reached out like that, eager to be held and lifted from their beds?

I remembered my daughter, soon after she learned to walk, calling me from her room. Lying in bed, she held her worn, yellow blanket to her mouth, and with the other outstretched arm, wiggled her fingers for me to come toward her. As I picked her up, she wound her little hands around my neck and her legs around my chest, nestling affectionately into my body. I felt a strong sense of security in a loving relationship that I believed would last forever. I didn't want to let her go. Now, facing my dying mother, I became anxious, realizing how transitory these feelings are.

I drew back the covers, wrapped my arms around my mother's back for support, and pulled her to an upright position. Then, with her limp arms around my neck, I swung both her legs over the side of the bed. Her struggle with this simple maneuver was so great that we had to wait several minutes for her to regain her breath. At her signal, I interlaced my arms around her and lifted her. She was barely able to support herself on her wobbly legs. It took all her energy to gain balance. She motioned for me to stand at her side and gently placed her arm through mine.

We walked together in tentative, slow steps toward the bathroom across the hall, I in my white T-shirt and boxer shorts and she in her yellow and pink pajamas. Our steps were carefully regulated as I tried to attune myself to her rhythm. Her walk was orderly and felt oddly formal, with a defined pause after each step. I flashed back to my wedding ceremony, walking down the aisle in rehearsed steps. My wife had whispered, "Slowly, slowly." Now, in the middle of the night, my mother was chanting the same word to me, "Slowly, slowly."

Four months earlier, at age seventy-seven, she had been diagnosed with pancreatic cancer, a basically untreatable disease. Up to that day, she was healthy, active, and self-sufficient. She had been widowed twice. Her last husband had died of emphysema, which had incapacitated him for more than two years. My mother became his nurse, but when he could no longer breathe with the oxygen tanks at home, she took him to the hospital, where he died within a week. After her loss, I was worried that she would become lonely and despondent. But within a few months, she confided in me with a rare openness, "Clem, I am the happiest I have been since the war. I don't have to take care of anybody except myself. I feel free. I feel good." She felt no guilt, nor was she embarrassed to say this. I was relieved and happy that my mother felt so light-hearted, and I cherished that moment, when I experienced a simple and unencumbered connection with her.

She then lived alone and free, as she wanted, for sixteen years. When the cancer struck, she was not stunned by this bodily assault. In fact, she was resolute in dealing with it on her own. She refused my suggestion to move into my house. My arguments and my pleading were useless. It was only when she became too physically weak to remain independent that she finally relented and came to live with me. While I truly wanted her to move, her change of mind signaled a defeat for her, a resignation that I was unaccustomed to seeing in her. My "success" made me sad.

Inside the bathroom, I helped my mother turn around at the toilet. Then I did something I never imagined I would do: I helped my mother pull her underpants down. I had no choice—she was staggering in her efforts to pull them down with one hand while grasping my arm with the other. Sitting on the toilet, she pointed to the water faucet, which I immediately turned on so it would trickle. When everything was in place, I stepped out, closed the door to give her privacy, and waited outside. I heard the water flowing in the sink. I thought, how many times did I do that for my children to help them pee in the potty?

When my son and daughter were learning to walk, they had clutched my hand for dear life while they swayed and lurched, not unlike my mother was doing now. But my children were loud, vigorous, and inspired. There was joy and laughter and the thrill of victory when they stood on their own small feet. I was thrilled by their excitement because it was the beginning of a whole big lifetime. My mother's victory, to stand momentarily on her own two feet, saddened me, as it signaled a life drawing to a close.

At that moment I felt time contract, and my lifespan narrow. I felt weary, and old myself. In the dim light, I saw the books collected over many years, the pictures of friends and family on the walls, of my kids joyously skiing down mountains, sailing boats, and celebrating birthday parties. All these wonderful memories that once made me smile were reduced to foreign artifacts. Even in my own home, I felt a cold detachment, like I was a visitor to a museum.

Time sweeps mercilessly over everything, and I wondered how much longer before I, too, would need my children to help me. I watched my life slide away from me. I felt my strength ebbing. On the timeline drawn from birth to death, I stood near the very end, along the edge of the cliff, about to fall into an abyss. Waves of darkness appeared all around me that I did not want to face.

I thought of how humiliating this must be for my mother, who measured her independence in terms of her success in avoiding being a burden others. My twenty-two-year-old daughter saw her grandmother's illness as a tragedy because my mother is the heroine of our family. My mother survived the Holocaust. She was twenty-two when the war started. Within two years, the Nazis nearly destroyed her entire foundation by killing her husband (my father), her mother, and her father in concentration camps. She stood alone and homeless during the war, but she took care of me and saved her brother's life. Day and night for five years, she was always one step ahead of the Nazis. She escaped a concentration camp, and she found a convent that kept me safe while she, under forged Catholic papers, worked as a nanny for Polish and German families. In one of her most daring moves, my mother obtained a job as a nanny for a Gestapo family. I pictured her strolling down a Warsaw promenade with a blond, blue-eyed child and a German shepherd by her side. Who would challenge this disguise?

When the war ended, she emerged from the nightmare and smoke with pride for not just surviving, but for having outwitted the Nazis and saving me. But survival in that constant and relentless threat created profound anxiety and demanded acute vigilance. It was in this anxious and alert state that she entered the new world. And although the world into which she was stepping offered fresh hope for safety, any expectations were darkened by the war.

I loved and admired my mother. In her terrible trauma, she had become a keen witness to a noxious history. She could reach inside herself for the most painful memories and with the composure of a reporter provide names, dates, and places. If the memories were too painful, she would say, "Not now, ask me later." There was seldom a "later," because some experiences were too hurtful to recall, and I felt too nervous to ask about them.

She assumed, and I believe welcomed, the position of family historian. Sometimes I thought of her as a rabbi with whom the family sought an audience. Her brother, his wife, their children, and my children would all come to her to resolve questions of memory.

We all had questions: "When did you return to the convent to get your son? And is it true that he was in the convent three to six months?" "No," my mother would answer. "He lived there for two years. He wouldn't be here if I hadn't been lucky enough to place him. After I was liberated in March 1945, I went back to the convent to get him. I didn't even know if he was alive. I remember I arrived in the afternoon. Maria, a kind nun he liked, opened the door and told me that he was safe."

As easy as it was for my mother to recall past events, it was as hard to find her emotional inner life. Her anguish and fragility were familiar to those close to her but hidden behind a screen and difficult to touch. I wondered if anyone could reach her. She seldom talked to me about my father or our past unless I asked about something specific. I had begun to understand only recently that she never recovered from the horror of the war. She did not have more children; she did not finish her studies in dentistry; she did not resume playing the piano; and she remained secretive and vigilant—two qualities that had served her well during the war. I felt puzzled that she refused to tell anyone outside her immediate family about her illness. She insisted on privacy till the very end.

I heard my name called from the bathroom. I went in and helped my mother get up from the toilet and dress. We then returned to her room in the same way, with Mother holding my arm tightly. I helped her turn and sit on the edge of the bed. I waited for her breathing to calm. Then she let herself fall back on the pillows as I lifted her legs onto the bed and covered her. Exhausted from this short trip across the hallway, she gasped for more air. When her breathing returned to normal, she gathered her strength and said clearly and loudly, "Thank you." I was surprised by the formality in her tone and felt strange that she needed to thank me for merely helping her across the hall.

One day, I suggested to Mother that soon she would be in heaven. At first, she shrugged her shoulders, but I pressed and said that maybe my father was in heaven, and she could reunite with him. She looked thoughtfully into my eyes and after a long pause said, "It's too crowded up there." I laughed. She never did like crowds. But I have always wondered what she really meant by that. Did she mean that there are too many Holocaust victims in heaven?

Days later, I was standing in front of the window watching a tugboat pushing a barge up the Hudson River, when my son called from my mother's room and said, "Dad, I think Grandma stopped breathing." I didn't hurry to my mother. I walked slowly, almost deliberately. I then did what the hospice nurse instructed me to do: I checked her pulse, I placed my ear by her mouth to listen for any breath, and as a final precaution, I held a mirror under her nose. There was no condensation; the mirror was clear.

I did not weep, nor did I feel much, except a kind of diffused tension that accompanies fear. I felt cold, like my mother was now. I felt strangely detached from my grief, which settled a few feet away from me, like puddles of water that would form outside my house after a rainstorm. Nevertheless, I knew that if I wanted to, I could reach those feelings again.

My daughter announced that my mother was gone. She imagined that she had seen a blue mist lift from her grandmother's body, and that my mother had now entered a tunnel in which a white light drew her into a spiritual world. There, my daughter thought, she could reside in peace and safety.

I called the nurse, and within a half hour, she arrived and pronounced my mother dead. She signed the death certificate, expressed her sympathy, and indicated that I should now call the funeral home. On the way out, she must have mentioned to the doorman that my mother had died.

Within minutes of the nurse leaving, the doorbell rang, and a young policeman stood in the doorway. He was in full uniform and armed. His formality alarmed me because he looked like he had come to my house on some very serious business. "I understand there is a dying person in this apartment," he said.

"No, she is dead already. Why are you here?"

"I was called—"

"By whom? I didn't call the police."

Uninvited, he forced himself past me and said, "Where is she?"

"'She is my mother, and she is in bed... dead."

"How do you know she is dead? Who certified her death?"

"The hospice nurse."

"The who?" he asked, as if he didn't know the meaning of the word "hospice."

I found the exchange with the policeman very unnerving. For a moment, his features looked Aryan, and I felt a jolt come over me. At this moment, I felt detached and without a will of my own. Yet—and this is the strange thing about it—I felt safe.

I explained, "The hospice nurse is the woman who took care of her while she was dying."

"The only person qualified to pronounce her dead is the medical examiner. Was he called?"

"No, but—"

"Then I have to get the medical examiner here." He was looking around the room. His eyes narrowed and he asked, "Where are all the drugs she used?"

Without thinking, I said, "Oh, I dumped most of them in the toilet, so no one would take them by mistake."

"You threw them out? You can't destroy evidence!" He walked over to the bathroom and looked into the toilet. "Did you flush them?"

"Yes. Evidence? What evidence? Is this a criminal investigation? What, are you thinking that I killed my mother? Am I a suspect?" I yelled at him. Why was I even talking to him? I must have lost my mind.

The cop's cold eyes caused a shudder of fear to pass through me. I saw in him a hollow arrogance that denied the presence of my mother, my children, or me. He was a cop with a duty to perform. Nothing else mattered.

The doorbell rang. Two burly men dressed in black were waiting for me.

"Good evening. We are from the funeral home. I understand you called us."

"Yes, I did."

"Can we come in?" I let them in and pointed to Mother's room.

One of the men wore a suit about two sizes too small. His white shirt protruded from his sleeves and covered half his hands. When he walked down the hallway, his shoulders almost touched each wall.

The cop saw him coming. "Who is that?" He demanded. Before anyone could answer, the cop said, "Please, stay back. No one removes anything or anyone from this site before the medical examiner gets here."

"But I am the undertaker. I was asked by the woman's son to—"

"I don't care who asked you."

Thinking they would come to blows, I stepped between them. I pushed the undertaker back into the living room and tried to calm him. I asked him to sit and wait with his partner.

I returned to the cop, who was still looking over my mother's room. With the covers pulled up to her neck, she looked peaceful, like she was sleeping. I wondered what she would have thought about all of this.

Instead of experiencing myself contracting as I did when the cop intruded, I now felt myself expanding, as if touched by my mother's spirit. I felt like I was emerging from the clouds, out of the past, into the present. I now felt bigger and taller, and I occupied more space than the cop did.

"Listen," I said firmly. "This certificate is legit. I want you to call the doctor at the hospital and verify it."

"No, only the medical coroner can do that."

"OK, then call him. Call him now! And get out of this room." I still felt awkward, and was suspended between laughter and fury. When I found my rage, which took the form of contempt, I pushed him out of my mother's room, without touching him. I stared into his cold eyes and moved steadily but slowly closer to him. As I moved forward, he slowly retreated out of the room and toward a phone to call the medical examiner's office.

The doorbell rang once again. Two hefty female paramedics stood in the doorframe with oxygen tanks, backpacks, and other life-support equipment on their shoulders. They told me they had been called to help a dying woman. I said, "You must have the wrong house, because my mother already died."

They looked at the number on the door. "Well, no, this is the right place. Your doorman called the police, and they called us. Once the call is made, we are required to check it out."

"I already have a cop and two frustrated undertakers in here."

"Look, we are sorry, but we have to go in," they said.

I let them in and showed them my mother. I told the paramedics that my mother had died and that a hospice nurse had certified her death, but that the policeman was not accepting this. They understood, but nevertheless checked my mother, looked at the certificate, then told the cop that my mother was indeed dead and that the certificate was legitimate. The cop grumbled something and shook his head, turning his attention back to the phone. The paramedics left, confused.

When the cop hung up the phone, he reported that they couldn't find the examiner.

He paced back and forth, trying to figure out his next move. Finally, he called his superior, who must have reprimanded him, because he looked humbled for the first time since he barged in.

"I was just doing my job here," he said, and turned to me without making eye contact. "Everything is in order now. You can do what you want." And without apologies, he walked out the door.

Before I told the undertakers to proceed, I took one more look at my mother. In death, she had just witnessed, once again, the bizarre and incomprehensible. I don't know why, but I checked to see whether her expression had changed. It hadn't.

I stood alone by my mother's side in silence. The room was quiet. I felt an admiration for her for saving our lives and a pure gratitude that only happens at the moment when any other expectations are not possible. I thought of her puzzling "thank you" for helping her cross the hallway. So, I said, "Thank *you*, and goodbye, Mom."

I walked out to join my son and daughter in the living room. I didn't want to see the undertakers carrying my mother out in a bag. The three of us went to the window and watched another tugboat push its cargo slowly up the Hudson. I heard a voice in back of me say "Goodbye," and the door slammed.

A Quarter for Coffee

A black man was shadow boxing, zig-zagging down the sidewalk in his unlaced, ankle-high shoes, putting on a show, hopeful for a donation. He was slim, medium height, and shorter than me. His stained khaki pants drooped below his waist, which was covered by a black T-shirt. His cheeks sunk in to fill the space of teeth probably knocked out in fights, and his air punches were so threatening that the crowd of people parted, clearing a path for his uneven gait. His fists were big for his size, with swollen, scarred knuckles. He must have been a boxer in his younger days, or maybe a sparring partner. I saw in his eyes something ironic, as if he were amused by the repelling effect he had on people. He seemed to observe himself and others from far away, like he was doing something crazy on purpose, like he was pretending to be drunker and crazier than he really was. Strangely, I felt a kinship with him and didn't feel frightened.

My friend Stanley and I had been rambling through the always-bustling Greenwich Village that night, looking at girls, hoping to get lucky. Every time I went to the Village I was hoping to get lucky. Breathing in the neighborhood air when I came out of the subway, I experienced the Village as an aphrodisiac, with its air of sex and jazz.

I scanned the packed streets for pretty girls, trying to catch their eye. But the only eyes that looked back at me belonged to a guy who was smiling, hoping that he'd get lucky, too. Across the street, I caught sight of an amazing-looking woman marching down the street, with a bounce so light it seemed like she was walking on a trampoline. She was dressed in brown leather pants and a tight jacket with boots, her blond hair flowing down her back. I elbowed Stanley. We crossed the street to follow her. She stepped into a coffeehouse, and we secretly watched her through the glass. As she sat at a small, round table and ordered something, my excitement was curbed by fear. Stanley nudged me. "Go ahead. She's alone, probably wants to be picked up. I'll wait here."

My nerves followed me as I entered the coffeehouse and strode straight toward her. I leaned on the empty chair next to her and stammered, "Do you mind if I join you for some coffee?"

Her beautiful, green eyes shifted from staring into space to focus on my face, and with a chilling, clear voice, snapped, "Why don't you go masturbate in the corner?"

On the way out, Stanley asked me what happened. Too dazed to speak, I mumbled to myself, "That bitch," and we walked on. I felt too humiliated to talk about it.

It was a warm evening in June, but in the jammed streets of the Village, it felt hot. We made our way toward the Village Vanguard, where I was eager to hear Charlie Mingus play. I hoped I'd even see him lose his temper and smash his bass into the ceiling light, as I heard he'd done before. It seemed like jazz was everywhere, inside the clubs and out on the street. From a second-floor window, I could hear what sounded like

John Coltrane on his tenor saxophone, playing the new Hard Bob style, a mixture of rhythm and blues and gospel music. With its tones and rhythms, jazz, particularly the saxophone, had the power to fly me somewhere I had never been before, somewhere where everything was fresh and unscathed. The beat shook and twisted my body, and the pleasure was so profound that I felt like I was playing the instrument, and the sound originated within me.

In the Village, I saw people behave freely, without fear of retribution. They could dress sloppy, like hipsters on the street, or be unshaven and have long hair, even walk barefoot. Meanwhile, I was still being careful not to stand out; I always tried to blend in with the crowd. I saw a couple kissing, he in shorts and T-shirt, she in a flowery dress, both leaning against a street door. His hand was about to slip under her loose dress. I was a voyeur, taking pleasure in watching others who did as they wished. To be able to speak, behave, and think freely was enticing yet still so novel that it was hard for me to embrace it. The atmospheric buzz of the Village, like improvisational jazz, was the antidote to hiding.

That night in the Village, in 1956, Stanley was walking on my right. His freshly greased, wavy hair, combed straight back, exposed big black eyes that were wider set than those of other boys. His nose was flat, the bottom wide, probably to balance his eyes. He had a calm and composed charm, with a Bulgarian accent that spiced up his appeal to girls.

The black man must have seen me watching him because he paused his routine and asked, "Do you have a quarter for a cup of coffee?"

I was in good spirits, buoyed by my friend's jocular mood.

I responded, "For coffee? You're going to collect a bunch of money and buy more booze, not coffee!"

"Naw. I want coffee, man."

"Oh, come on, I don't believe you. You're just out for drinks." I was nervous. Yet there was something kind in his eyes that allowed me to step over my anxiety. He came closer and stared into my eyes like he might have done in the ring, staring down his opponent before a fight. I blinked first. He won. Then he slowly walked around me from left to right, constantly keeping his eye on me. I stood still, waiting for him to face me again. When he came around, he stepped closer to me, looked into my eyes, and with his liquor-drenched breath, said, "You're a Jew, ain't you?"

I looked him straight in the eyes and without thought, said, "And you're a nigger, ain't you?"

Stanley's eyes got even bigger, and his mouth opened. I was momentarily suspended, waiting for something big to happen. It was as if we were both stunned by a wicked punch. Still, I knew that if he were to hit me, I'd be hurt. Rooted in that moment was a fear of death and the deep humiliation that comes from having once been forced to hide my identity. I thought of myself as a shame-filled child walking through alleys and staying close to shadows of buildings for fear of being found out. As much as I felt helpless facing this man, I also felt empowered by confronting the person who called me the very word that had marked me as "other." Here, in Greenwich

Village, New York, I was both the victim and the aggressor, as was he.

Then, as quickly as we had exchanged our verbal blows, the boxer and I simultaneously relaxed, smiled at each other, and reached out to shake hands. His was strong and sandpaper- rough as he wrapped it around my smaller hand. We stood face to face trying to make sense of what had just happened. I felt my shoulders drop and my body unwrap from tension. I felt relieved and so deeply moved. I maintained my steady look. Staring into his eyes I quietly asked, "How about I buy you a drink?"

He looked startled by my offer but said, "Yeah. OK."

The three of us entered the nearest tavern and sat at a square table opposite the bar. The waiter came over, and I ordered three beers.

"Sorry, but you can only have two."

"Why?"

"Because we don't serve drunks!"

I looked at my new companion for his reaction, but his expression was flat.

"OK, then, two beers and one coffee," I said, slapping my hand on the table.

The Blue-Green Circle

I was sitting in a New York City diner having a grilled cheese sandwich and coffee, listening to Eddie tell me about his trip to Ukraine in a few months. It was 1997.

"I go there every two years," he said.

"Since the war ended? That many times?"

"No, I started in the '50s."

Eddie, as a child, had been hidden by a Christian family during the Holocaust. The rescuing mother was twenty-five, with children of her own, when she accepted him as her son. He was eight. Now he goes to help the elderly woman, who has grandchildren. He has bought them basic household things, including a stove and blankets, and pays for their utilities.

"You want to come?"

"No, I don't think so. I have no urge to return to Poland. Haven't even thought about it. But I understand your going. You are generous in giving back to this family. I have no one to go back to."

The town where I was born was part of Poland. Now it's part of Ukraine.

"Could be good," he pressed. "I can help you find the house where you were born."

After reflecting for a few days, I realized that I wanted to get a sense of my father, who I don't really remember. He was only thirty-two when he was killed by the Nazis, and I was four. I wanted to get a sense of the town and of the house I was born in. I hoped that my father and grandparents would come alive for me, and I would connect with all of them in some way. I called my daughter and told her about Eddie's proposition. Jennifer had finished college and was working as a documentary filmmaker.

"Hmm," she said. "We could piggyback on his trip. I could borrow a video camera and film it. Let's do it, Dad. If you're OK with it."

Because of Jennifer's support and enthusiasm about the trip, I started to get excited. I wouldn't go on my own, but Eddie knew the area and spoke Russian, Ukrainian, and Polish. A guide who is a friend and speaks all these languages? How lucky could I be?

Another friend heard about my upcoming trip and gave me a mezuzah. He told me, "You can leave this mezuzah in Poland as a remembrance of your father."

Before we left, I gathered my son and daughter and asked them to write a short note to the grandfather they never met. I told them I would put the notes into the mezuzah. And that I wanted to have a symbolic burial for him in his hometown and my place of birth. They knew my father had been gassed in the Belzec camp when I was four. The expressions on their faces were thoughtful and solemn, trying to figure out how to deal with my request. The silence continued as each of us began to write within our own private space: "Dear Dad," I began and started to cry. As far as I remembered, I had never uttered, wrote, or called anyone "Dad." I sat motionless, waiting for my feelings to settle and my eyes to dry. Then I wrote:

Dear Dad,

You must have been a good father because I have loving memories of you. I am sorry you couldn't live a longer life. I missed you. And I am sorry you couldn't enjoy your wonderful grandchildren. I hope your soul is in peace and that you are now with Mom, the woman you have always loved.

Love, your son, Klemak.

My son wrote:

Dear Olesh,

I send you blessings and wish that you finally have peace. I am sorry that I didn't know you.

Love, Shannon.

My daughter wrote:

Dear Olesh,

I am sorry we never got to meet you. Thank you for giving us such a wonderful father.

Love, Jennifer.

I folded the three papers into the smallest pieces I could and inserted them into the mezuzah.

My son was unable to go, but Jennifer, Eddie, and I flew to Frankfurt, Germany, and then took Ukrainian Air to Lvov, in Ukraine. Security at the airport felt like a war zone. Soldiers wearing dark gray uniforms and holding drawn machine guns wandered around like aimless ants. With grim faces, their searching eyes gazed at everyone and every piece of baggage. The line moved slowly and quietly, making me uneasy. I looked at my daughter to sense how she felt. We forced a smile at each other.

The immigration officer asked, "What is the purpose of your visit—business or pleasure?"

"Pleasure. I was born nearby and came back to see the town for the first time since I was a child," I answered.

"Just pleasure? Any other reason?"

"No, no other reason."

"What town were you born in?"

"Stanisławów."

"That is no longer the name. Now it's Ukrainian—called Ivano-Frankivsk."

"Yes, that's what I heard. Named after a Ukrainian poet." I was getting more and more polite out of nervousness. He showed a little smile, looked me and my daughter straight in the eyes, as if he could find something behind them, and then he punched our passports.

Before the war, Lvov had been a major Polish and Jewish cultural center. It has maintained the feel of culture and charm, with its old, well-preserved gothic buildings and cobblestone roads. I looked at the strangers on the street, wondering who— or whose family—may have been involved in the pogroms, as killers or collaborators. I tried to be open-minded, but this suspicion kept coming up, even though the faces I saw were ordinary and gave no sign of validating my suspicions.

We ate our dinner in town at a large, barren restaurant, with columns in the corners as the only remnants of prewar architecture. Most of the white-clothed tables were empty. Waiters stood erect against the wall, waiting for diners. I ordered borscht to start, then boiled pierogi filled with potatoes and cheese. My daughter did the same. My mother used to make pierogi from scratch, and the taste brought warm sensations to me.

In the morning, Eddie arranged for a man to pick us up and drive 100 miles south to my hometown. The driver was a thin man with a wrinkled face, kindly eyes, and persistent smile. He bowed frequently when talking to us, gesturing as if he were our servant. He spoke some English but was fluent in Polish, Russian, and Ukrainian. Eddie had mentioned that he was Jewish, born at the end of the war in Ukraine. His family had survived and stayed on after the war. "Incredible that his family stayed behind," I whispered to my daughter. "Ukrainians were the most hostile to Jews and eager collaborators with the Nazis. And they made their own pogroms, too, without the Nazis."

The driver was cautious about what he expressed. He spoke only when spoken to and then mostly in monosyllables. Yet he always had a smile on his face. Sitting in the back of his black Volga sedan was scary. It must have been thirty years old, battered by a long succession of owners. It was covered with dents and rusty blotches that reminded me of an abstract painting. Inside the car, I noticed that a piece of the floor in back was missing. I could see the blurry road below me. I was surprised that the car still moved. Our driver was careful to observe speed limits, or perhaps it was just that the car couldn't go faster.

When we got to my town, I looked out the window, straining to recognize something.

"Anything look familiar to you?" my daughter and Eddie frequently asked. This would become a refrain. My answer was always a puzzled expression. I felt dumb and powerless, straining to recreate a slice of memory.

Our hotel was a three-story, gray-and-white wooden structure with a black awning in front. It was clean and simple. The bathroom was well maintained and smelled fresh; it was stocked with plenty of toilet paper, and the toilet worked. The woman behind the desk spoke English, but Eddie had to translate to almost everyone else.

We went out to eat at a restaurant recommended by the hotel. The bare, wooden tables reminded me of a college cafeteria. We ordered classic local food: borscht, served with chopped eggs and sour cream floating on top; salad made of beets, shredded chopped potatoes, and vegetables; and roasted lamb. The potato pancakes, one of my favorites when Mother made them, were soggy.

Toward the end of the meal, I went to the bathroom, opened the door, and was assaulted by a putrid smell. The toilet was piled high with crap. There was no flushing or sewer connection, a common condition in restaurants, I learned. Where do people go? I rushed outside, found some bushes to hide me, and peed, scared that I'd be arrested. After that, we chose restaurants based on the condition of their toilet facilities.

Eddie would call, and in Ukrainian say, "I'd like a reservation for three, please."

Then, when they confirmed the reservation, he'd be sure to ask, "Does your toilet work?"

One evening, we sat at a table in the hotel bar. It was a pleasant atmosphere, and people seemed friendly. Eddie ordered vodka for me, wine for my daughter, and soda for himself. A group of people came in—two beautiful, tall blondes accompanied by three men. Eddie leaned over and told me that they were Ukrainians who had been robbed on the highway; they drove a Mercedes. They said there were highway bandits on the road, especially at night. The atmosphere felt like the Wild West. The fear of the locals made my own fear rise. I was glad I wasn't driving a car.

Our driver picked us up in the morning to drive us to the local rabbi, who would take us to the cemetery. The rabbi was in his early forties, medium height, with a stout body. His black beard matched his black suit and vest and round, black hat. Everything was so well coordinated and fit so perfectly that it looked like he had been born in the clothes he wore. His eyes met mine with a friendly welcome. Although he spoke some English, he preferred Ukrainian, so Eddie translated for us.

I told him what I wanted. He took his bible and a portable shovel with a handle that folded in half. We squeezed into our car and drove to the cemetery.

In the field in front of the graves, we crossed a faded blue-green line about a foot wide.

"What's this blue-green line, Rabbi?" I asked.

"The Germans executed Jews and buried them in this mass grave. There was so much blood around, they sprayed a disinfectant around the grave to hide the blood and prevent disease from spreading. They forbid anyone to go inside the line."

"This must be a huge grave. Who dug it out?" my daughter asked.

"I don't know, but probably Ukrainians or Jews before they were shot."

I remembered the scariest movie I ever saw, while I was in high school. It was called *The Thing*. In an American outpost in freezing Antarctica, during the night hours, scientists hear an ice-splitting crash that shakes their barracks. They go outside with flashlights and see nothing. Strange: since the crash was so big, there had to be something. The captain says, "I see a shiny, metallic object under the ice. Must be some sort of aircraft."

They are puzzled by the shape and size. The captain tells the men to stand on the edge of what they see. About a dozen people move around, until each one stands on the edge of this aircraft. The shape they form is round.

"Looks like something from outer space, probably a flying saucer!" someone shouts. They dig it out of the ice and discover a huge frozen monster inside. They keep the monster frozen by cutting out a rectangular shape in the ice around its body. They bring this huge ice piece inside. A guard is assigned to watch. But he gets spooked and covers the iced "thing" with a blanket, while he watches a show on a black-and-white TV. The ice slowly drips and melts under the blanket. The monster wakes, escapes, and goes on a killing spree.

Here, at the graveside, I asked that we spread out and stand on the blue-green line. When we stopped, I realized that we had formed a circle. There was thirty feet of space between me and Jennifer, who stood opposite me.

"How many Jews were killed here, Rabbi?" I asked.

"I don't know. Many thousands. There are many mass graves."

I stepped inside the circle and felt a tremor in my body. I feared the ground under me would collapse and I'd fall on top of aged corpses, cracking their skeletons. Above us and to the right, a pair of black and gray hawks perched motionless on leafless branches. They stared at us, waiting for a piece of flesh to pounce on.

Nature expressed our sorrow. Dark clouds hovered overhead. The obstructed sun, unable to form shadows of the trees, tombstones, or us, rendered the landscape flat and forlorn. We were the only people in the run-down cemetery. Inscriptions on headstones were barely visible. Some headstones sunk into the ground as if they were absorbed by quicksand. Most of the tombstones were knocked down, while some were partially broken or cracked. This was the town's old Jewish cemetery. When I was born, just before the war, there were thirty thousand Jews in my town. Now, the estimate had collapsed to about three hundred.

"The vandals sometimes dig out the graves to steal money or jewelry from the skeletons," the rabbi said.

"Jewelry?" I asked with astonishment.

"Yes, they didn't know that Jews were forced to undress and turn over their valuables before the mass shootings. The vandals thought they'd find jewelry on their bodies. Some may have found jewelry; most didn't. Others pulled gold off the bodies' teeth." He paused to calm himself, and continued. "Only recently have the police cracked down on them."

"Why the mass shootings? Didn't they have extermination camps?" Jennifer asked while rolling her camera.

"In the Stanisławów region, the Germans wanted to exterminate the Jews before the camps were built. They were in a hurry. There was a day in October 1941 called Bloody Sunday when Germans wanted to solve the 'Jewish Question.' They killed thousands that day." He spoke Polish now. Eddie translated. The rabbi's vibrant eyes lost their sparkle, and his expression of sorrow shifted to blankness. It was as if he had momentarily left his body. I, in turn, felt suspended, losing track of where I was and who I was with. My shoulders slumped forward in defeat.

The moment passed, and I walked slowly, one step at a time, as if I were on a tightrope, into the area of the individual graves. The others followed, though I was unaware of their presence. I looked for a safe place to bury the mezuzah. I found a half-cracked tombstone and began to dig next to it with the small shovel that the rabbi had brought. I figured that vandals had already done their job here, so they were unlikely to return.

After a bit, I asked my daughter if she'd like to dig, too. She handed me the camera, and I filmed her as she dug. When she was finished, she took the camera back from me, and I placed the mezuzah inside the hole we had dug. The rabbi motioned to me that this was the time for him to say the kaddish, the prayer for the dead. I put a black yarmulke on my head and the rabbi lead the kaddish, which I recited with him.

Yitgaddal veyitqaddash shmeh rabba. May God's great name be exalted and sanctified.

When he finished, we all said "Amen."

I covered the little grave, patted it down with my hands, stood up, and spoke to some invisible spirit I hoped was watching or listening.

"Dear Father, I am very sorry we all lost you so early in your life. I wish you would have been with me. And I wish you could have seen your grandchildren. You would have thought they were great, and they would have loved you, too. I am sorry we were not able to have a burial for you. But we are having it now. I hope you will finally reunite with my mother, the woman you loved. Goodbye, Dad. We love you. Amen."

The birds continued their pestering with their impatient, shrill whistles and whining calls. With no breeze to push them, the clouds stood still, as did the leaves on the bushes. I handed the shovel back to the rabbi. He folded it, and we left.

We returned to his office for my second mission—for the rabbi to help me locate the house that my grandfather built and in which I was born. He showed us some documents he found in the city hall that provided evidence of the ownership of the house.

Throughout the trip to Stanisławów, I tried to prod my memory for any fragment of past experiences in this town. I searched for a smell, a voice, or a vision that would spark such a memory. I felt the strain of that pressure, feeling tired and needing to pump myself up every day.

Before the visit to the house, I wanted to stop at a place where my uncle told me Mother would sometimes take me for a walk. We drove to the small lake near the house. There, along the edge of the water, was a concrete walkway that made a long, rectangular loop around a raised divide in the middle. Here we found couples strolling, with the women holding onto the men's arms, women walking with their children, and singles perhaps searching for a friend. They walked counter-clockwise, circling in unison around the elongated garden filled with bushes and flowers.

I was looking for a boy who was about three or four years old, to get a sense of how small I was when my family was forced out of our home and into a ghetto. I tried to imagine my mother walking with me here, holding my hand. I saw several mothers pass me, holding their child's hand. Feeling awkward, I stopped one of them.

"Excuse me, can I ask you how old your child is? I was born here."

The first woman ignored me, probably frightened by a stranger speaking English, and walked on without looking at me. Another woman I stopped told me her child was seven.

On the third try, a woman in her twenties stopped and turned to me. I repeated the question, and in slow, halting English, she responded, "My child is four years old." I explained to her as simply as I could my purpose in visiting here and that I was her son's age when this was Poland. She smiled, and in a heavy Slavic accent said something encouraging that I couldn't understand. "*Dzienkuje*," I said, as I thanked her in Polish with one of the few words I still remembered.

"*Witac*," she responded with a smile—the word she uttered had sounded like "welcome"—and continued her stroll, holding her son's hand. I watched them carefully walk away.

He looked happy. What a shock he'd have if tomorrow his family was ordered by the police to leave home and they were pushed into an overcrowded ghetto.

I thought I would remember being held by my father or mother on this common walkway. Not even a fragment of an image came to me. But I felt a new compassion for myself, seeing how small and vulnerable I must have been when I was marched into the town's ghetto.

Meanwhile, Jennifer was always filming.

The rabbi told me our house was located on Lipowa Street, number 6 or 8. The buildings on that block were stacked side by side. They were similar to townhouses in New York, but the fronts of the stone houses were flat and exactly flush with each other, looking like one continuous three-story building. We weren't sure which house was mine. There was also a "6A" address, to further confuse me.

I called my uncle in Chicago, who had been eighteen at the time, to ask him if he remembered the number of our house. He didn't. But he did remember that the house had a balcony in front with a partition on the right side.

I returned to Lupowa Street. Did he mean "right" from the street or "right" from the house? I went back and forth between the houses. I examined closely the entrance to a house with a balcony and partition. At the entrance, before I opened the door, high on the inside left wall, I noticed a dusty, dirt-covered, rectangular metal plate nailed to the wall. I cleaned it off and read that the house was built in 1935 by Joseph Low. That was my grandfather. I had finally found my house. It was number 6A.

The foyer was dim. Walking slowly up the five marble stairs to the first floor, I listened for my mother's voice telling me as a three year old to be careful as I crawled up the stairs. Or to hear my father's voice behind me, encouraging me to walk up one step at a time. But I heard nothing. I yearned for the smell of Mother's chicken soup or mushrooms, pan-cooked with sour cream and garlic. My nose detected nothing. Yet something about the dark entrance felt close to me. I waited for the fog of memory to lift. It never did.

The house was clean and in excellent shape inside. I was surprised that sixty-five years later the house was as solid as an entrance to an old stone church.

My parents' apartment had been on the first floor. My mother gave birth to me in the bedroom of that apartment. We knocked on the door to the right. Minutes passed. Then a gruff man's voice behind the door asked in Ukrainian, "What do you want?"

Eddie told him in Ukrainian about me, that I just came to look at the apartment that I lived in as a child.

When he heard that I was born here, he raised his voice even higher and yelled, "Get out, or I'll call the police."

Eddie pleaded with him, but he refused to open the door. I thought perhaps that he was afraid I would want to re-claim the apartment, as some have tried to do in other parts of Europe. We walked up to the second floor, where my mother's parents had lived with their son, my uncle. Jennifer continued filming while we knocked on the door. This time, a young, friendly couple greeted us. They invited us in and offered tea or water. They were renters, living in the apartment for two months while waiting to immigrate to America. I took panoramic photographs of the apartment, including the cylindrical water heater that stood near the kitchen. I didn't even try to remember anything about my grandparents' place.

When I returned to America, I showed the photos to my uncle. He could not believe that the furniture was exactly as he had remembered it before the war. I was amazed about the durability and condition of that whole house and furniture.

We left the house and dropped off the rabbi. On the way back to our hotel, while Jennifer was filming the countryside, we spotted two soldiers on our side of the road, waving an orange wand up and down like windshield wipers. Our driver told us nervously, "We must stop. They want to inspect us."

We pulled over and stopped in front of the two soldiers, who had machine guns hanging from their shoulders. They walked to either side of the car and looked us over. Across the road, two additional soldiers watched us. The driver got out of the car and spoke with one soldier as the other kept an eye on us. My daughter was in the front seat; I was in the back. I told her to put the camera on the floor.

Our driver returned, and through the window, he told us that they wanted the camera and film. "They think you are going to use the film as propaganda against Ukraine."

"Tell them that this is my daughter, and the filming is only for personal use. That I was born here and returned just for a visit."

He walked back to tell the soldier, but I could see by the soldier's arm movement that they didn't believe him. I got out of the car very slowly with palms of my hands exposed to them.

As I walked toward them, I could see that the two soldiers across the road drew their machine guns and walked briskly toward us. We now had four soldiers. I was oddly amused by all this attention, guns and all. It felt like a drug bust gone bad. We had nothing to hide. I repeated in quiet English to our driver what I had said earlier. I could see the soldiers getting more agitated. The driver told me that it would be best if I returned to the car. I did. We waited. The driver returned and said, "All right, you can keep the camera, but they want some money."

"How much?" I asked.

"Five dollars."

"How much?" I asked again, thinking he made a mistake.

"Five dollars," he repeated.

"OK, Dad. I have an idea," Jennifer said. "You go out and give them the five dollars, maybe even ten, and I will film it."

"Are you crazy? Put that camera down."

I handed the driver the five. He gave them the money. They stepped back from the road, lowered their machine guns, and waved us to go. We drove off to our hotel. The driver was quiet, but we chattered nonstop. I laughed about the absurdity of the incident, yet I felt relief, knowing that I would fly home the next day. At the entrance to the hotel, I tipped the driver well, in dollars. We all hugged him and expressed gratitude for his service. He smiled and bowed. I felt sad knowing that he was trapped in this town and that we were leaving him behind. Jen said, "Maybe he doesn't feel as bad as you."

On our last night, Eddie said he had some dance music tapes, so I invited him to our room and ordered vodka for all of us. Our room had two queen beds that I pushed together. I turned all the lights out, except for one table lamp that exuded a yellowish tint in the room. He put on Tito Puente, the king of Latin music, playing the salsa. He asked if he could dance with my daughter. I took the camera and filmed them. Before he started his real estate business, Eddie had been a dance instructor at a major ballroom studio in New York. Short and overweight, he didn't look like a dancer, but when he danced, he moved gracefully, almost as if he were floating. His body easily found the salsa rhythm and remained level. He led Jen around effortlessly side to side, swirled her one way, and then another. Then I handed the camera to Eddie and danced with my daughter, whose animated brown eyes and happy face made me smile.

The next morning, we flew back to New York City. Jennifer edited thirty hours of film into a fifty-eight-minute documentary. She called it *Dear Dad.*

Miracles

It had been a long time since I had seen Julia, who broke up with me online after a four-year relationship. Yes, she emailed me the news. The news was not unexpected. But by email! Isn't that how teenagers break up? It was the only way she could do it, she would tell me later.

In the two years since this strange break-up we had only spoken twice, and that was during the past month. We felt good enough about our conversations to make a date, and I was hopeful that we would resume something good, like we'd had. She said that through her dating experiences she'd realized I was the only man she really loved (and that included her former husband). I told her that I, too, still loved her, but I felt cautious about seeing her, not because I didn't want to, but because I didn't want to get hurt again. Our telephone talks were quite satisfying, with both of us acknowledging things we'd previously disowned. The most striking new thing she told me was that she always thought that I was a "miracle." It was one of those things people say to let you know they fully appreciate and admire the very essence of you. I fell silent for a moment, stunned by the meaning of what she said. I knew what she meant, and I knew that it came from her heart.

So, on that night, I was feeling good about our forthcoming date, a romantic evening I planned with dinner, followed by a cabaret in the Oak Room at the Algonquin Hotel. A young jazz singer reminiscent of Billie Holiday was performing. I even sang in the shower, belting out creaky-sounding notes to Frank Sinatra's legendary songs. I wanted to look particularly good. I picked out my favorite shirt and suit. My mind was buzzing with our fun history.

Julia had a wonderful laugh that was hearty and genuine. Sometimes she laughed so hard she folded over, throwing her head forward with hair flying in an act of exhilaration. The laughter could be about something funny I said. I made her laugh a lot. Sometimes she simply laughed *at* me. I got a kick out of her making fun of me because I sure teased her a lot. This playful badinage is what made for our steamy chemistry in bed.

We made love everywhere—on the stairs in my house, in our berth on a sailboat, and on the rug in my office. One time, we were vacationing at a British Virgin Islands resort, in a cabin on a hill overlooking the Caribbean and the bay. At that height, the breeze was always present, and I loved to feel the wind brushing my face. On the deck, late in the afternoons, we had drinks and watched the sun cool down and sink in back of the horizon.

One such afternoon, Julia was bending over to remove her sandals. She looked like a dancer with straight legs and ass pointing up to the ceiling. I couldn't help but rub myself against her behind. She stayed bent over, and we both started breathing heavily. I felt the blood rushing to harden me. She felt it, too, and moaned to my rise. We rushed out naked onto our porch, falling into the hammock, Julia landing on top of me. She had a mild temperament outside of bed, but in bed, she liked to make her pleasures heard. We had privacy on the deck. Except at this one moment, the maid was climbing the stairs to change towels. I didn't hear her, but Julia did. I was surprised to see Julia turn her head and yell with such authority, "Go away! Not now!" She was like an animal protecting her lair. I heard footsteps retreating down the stairs.

I was fascinated that she continued the rhythm of sex while at the same time shouting at the maid. Her raw emotions made me even harder. The longer we did it, the deeper the hammock stretched out, but we both finished before it reached the floor. I held on to her tightly as my body quivered in spasms. When I quieted down, she turned her back toward me, and we rested, still panting, with my arms and legs curled around her. In our stillness, I was lost in joy and felt at peace within myself; my mind was unusually quiet—not a common state for me. I felt the wind cross my back, while the front of my body stayed warm from our sticky sweat. By now, the sun was reaching its end. On its way down, it radiated deep, maroon colors.

* * *

The phone rang.

"Hi, it's Julia."

I knew right away something was wrong. "What's the matter?" I asked.

She started to cry, "My doctor called me," she said. "I have cancer again. Can you believe it?"

"I am sorry. Really, really sorry."

"I know you are. I know."

"What happened? I didn't know there was anything—"

"There was nothing. I had a routine test that I have had for seven years, you know, every four months since my last cancer. Last week, my doctor said she felt something hard under my arm. She said it was nothing, but she didn't want take any chances. So, she did a biopsy. And she just called me. I can't go through this again."

"Is it the same breast? But it's under the arms, not breast."

"The breasts have muscles that extend under the arms. So, yes, the same one. I can't do it again. But I don't want to die. I may have to have a double mastectomy."

"You are not dying. Not any more than the rest of us. Let's first see what the rest of the tests say."

"I have to do a CAT scan and a bone scan... it's horrible. If it spread through my body, I am going to die. I don't believe this is happening again. I didn't want to call you and cancel. I waited till the last minute. My sister is coming over. I am going to spend the night with her."

"Of course. You do what you need to take care of yourself."

I heard the bell ring in her house.

"It's my sister. I have to go. I am really scared this time."

"I know it's scary, but we will have another night. You are very resilient and gutsy. There is always another night. We'll talk later. Good night."

I was very conscious of not saying "goodbye."

I took a walk. I thought about my oldest friend who was now dying of lung cancer. I thought about my best friend, who abruptly and unexpectedly died of heart failure five years ago. We were like motorcycle buddies. I never laughed with anyone as happily as I did with him. And I don't think I ever will. We mostly laughed at the black absurdities of life.

I thought of other unexpected losses of people close to me. And, of course, I thought of the big losses from my own hell, the Holocaust. I was a child then, and I was lucky to get out alive with a fairly intact mind. A "Swiss-cheese mind," as my best friend called it. Less than one out of twenty children survived that war. And of that five percent, most of them were girls. Very few boys survived, because the boys could easily be identified as Jews. It didn't matter how good the false documents were or what he looked like. If a Nazi was suspicious, he'd order the boy to take his pants down and the Jewishness would be exposed.

Although it was miraculous that I escaped, I never thought of myself as a "miracle" until Julia said it.

But now I felt very sad, and I thought of myself as a "cursed miracle." Yes, I was alive, and I was healthy (as far as I knew), but the pain of losses only accumulated. And there was limited space left to tolerate any further losses. We all have our ceilings of tolerance, no? Rather than feeling lifted and comforted by being a "miracle," I felt doomed. I felt I was fated to witness personal losses that had now become overwhelming. The pain of the losses and fears of future losses, including Julia's, is what made me feel cursed.

I went to a spot near my house in New Jersey on top of the Palisades Cliffs that overlooks the George Washington Bridge. It's a magnificent sight. You can see the bridge traffic up close and even hear the cars hissing their way across. The bridge looked majestic and massive, like someone had purposely enlarged it for me. From where I stood, the bridge, with its steel cables holding up the two decks of heavy traffic, looked indestructible. I think of it as one of the world's greatest wonders.

I imagined building an apartment on top of one of those towers. With windows all around, I would have enviable panoramic views. What vistas I would have! Wow! Down the Hudson River, I would be able to see all of Manhattan and the entry to the New York harbor. Up the Hudson, I would be looking down at the tall, rocky cliffs that define the river walls. I would have a nest in the sky. A magnificent spot, I thought. I imagined the wind constantly blowing, so that I would not be able to open any windows. But I like the sound that the wind makes. I could hear the wind play mostly classical music, the kind that was unpredictable and dramatic, only occasionally soothing.

At that height, I would need a red, blinking light to warn planes and to keep the birds from crashing into my windows. To take me to my penthouse on the tip of the towers, I'd also need an elevator. The engineers could figure this out. The one thing I was concerned with was parking. Where would I park my car? And where would guests park their cars? They couldn't just leave the car on top of the bridge. That's the one problem that could not be solved, making the house improbable.

I gazed into the Hudson. The blue-gray water is always bluer upriver. Perhaps because it is cleaner and fresher farther north. How deep is the river below me? It must be at least twenty to thirty feet deep, maybe even fifty feet in the middle. Would the water be cold? Probably not too cold this time of year, the end of August. I stood on the edge of the cliffs, with the water right below me, the height equivalent to about a twenty-story building. It was dusk, that transition time that brings uncertainty and with it, feelings of desperation. It's not daylight and it's not night. This in-between time has always made it difficult to place myself. Do I belong in the nighttime or the daytime? Change frightens me.

As the sun got dimmer, my eyes were drawn to a large, spherical object floating in the sky. It was shiny and smooth, like a gigantic billiard ball. It wasn't spinning, but it moved very slowly, hovering above me to my right. Although it was hard to tell its color because the sky was getting dark, I could nevertheless clearly see its shape. It was perfectly round. To my bewilderment, the front of this object opened up. Or perhaps it was open all along. In it, I saw two couples, the younger pair standing in front of the older two. The four were all looking at me. I tried to focus on them. It may seem strange, but I was no longer frightened. On the contrary, I felt comforted by this sight.

The more the people looked at me, the more familiar they became. And then I recognized them, as clearly and quickly as a camera clicking a picture. The couple in front was my parents! My mother and father! The older couple in the rear was my grandfather and grandmother. The men and women embraced. They looked at ease, and comfortable. They gazed at me with soft, faint smiles. I felt at peace.

I longed to touch my family and to talk to them. I wondered if I could be transported to them. As if they read my thoughts, in the blink of an eye I was standing in front of my family. I recognized my mother but not my grandparents or father, who I only really remembered from photographs my mother had saved. I hugged all of them, especially my dad and mom. My parents and grandparents seemed comfortable and secure. Given the ugly deaths of my father and grandparents in the Holocaust, I was surprised to find all of them in good spirits and full of confidence. They were very happy to see me, their only son. We hugged each other. I had not seen them or been with them for over half a century, except in my dreams, where they sometimes appeared.

After a few minutes of hugging, they said I needed to return to my place and sent me back down. I was relieved by the security and confidence with which they let me go.

When I looked up from my spot on the ground, they were still smiling and waving goodbye to me. What was weird about my experience was not the phantasmal nature of the spherical object floating in space or the futuristic technology that could beam me up and down but that it all happened so ordinarily, so normally, as if I were going to college for the first time. I felt my family's love and warmth. I was surprised by their calm after not having seen me for so many years. They now drifted farther away until I saw a speck and then just the darkening night sky, ushering in the evening.

I turned away from the river and walked back home.

Hopalong Cassidy

My mind is like a bad neighborhood. I try not to go there by myself, especially at night. But still, I have not been a victim of my mind. On the contrary, I have been proactive and mostly successful in improving the neighborhood. I have used tools like the psychoanalytic couch, meditation, hypnosis, group work, and the latest, narrative writing. The latter is particularly valuable because it builds continuity to my past, fills gaps in my memories, and most importantly, opens doors to spaces that are often surprising and wonderfully cathartic.

Perhaps there are those who, after all these efforts to successfully calm their minds, can enjoy the sight of light and smell of fresh air that appears after a rain. Yet for me, I feel fated to face the shadows of my past, so that when the excitement of joy subsides—and there is much joy in my life—loneliness appears like the sand on the beach following low tide. It is in this solitude, when I wish for calmness, that the loneliness grows the loudest. In the hours of the evening, when I am alone, the vastness of my solitude grows to a point that is painful and sad, like the end of summer. I would gladly exchange it for any other state, or live a few feet apart from my mind.

On the weekends, when I am with Angela, I don't feel alone. The other Saturday in November, we drove up to my house in Connecticut armed with plastic bags filled with food. Late in the afternoon, I sliced prosciutto and "ugly" tomatoes along with freshly made, still-warm mozzarella. I covered it all with basil, oil, and black pepper. Angela arranged our feast in a circle on a large, white plate. We baked ciabatta bread; I love its crisp crust and the crackling sound it makes as I bite. I opened a bottle of Pinot Grigio. We were absorbed in eating and drinking and spoke little, except for occasional comments about the food and wine.

Looking outside, I felt the coolness in the air and in the colors. The trees were like chameleons, having changed from greens to reds, and oranges to pinks. The wind had begun to strip the trees of leaves, making them barren and unfriendly. The sky was gray, and the wind swirled the brown leaves on the ground up into the air, where they floated aimlessly until they dropped to the ground. Some leaves parachuted down to land gently on earth. Others stayed afloat on their own accord, without the wind's help, and flew like hang gliders powered by currents of air; they rolled up and down on the updrafts, making aerobatic loops. The grass was still green, but now it had to endure the weight of the crumbled leaves that the ash, locust, and maple trees dropped.

The wine warmed me. We sat on the couch in front of the fireplace, sipping.

I asked, "Can you tell me a fairy tale?"

"You mean make something up?"

"No, read me one, or tell me one from memory. Did you read any fairy tales as a child?"

"All the time. Russian, Polish, and German stories. There was a point when the library had no more fairy-tale books I hadn't read. I loved them. And you?"

When or where would I have read them? I thought. "I don't remember reading any or being read to. I don't miss the fairy tales, but I do miss that no one ever read to me. Or maybe I just don't remember anyone reading to me," I told her.

I slipped down a chute into my past, searching my mind for fairy tales that I could not find. My mother may have read to me before I was three years old. She had time; she didn't work. Once the Germans rounded us up for the ghetto in 1941, I doubt whether anyone read to me. At gunpoint, the Germans forced my whole family to evacuate our house and squeezed us into a small apartment with people I did not know. I was four years old. The ghetto was contained within a six-square-block boundary. Most of us slept on the floor. I don't remember any books. Time and energy were devoted to surviving, planning escapes, getting food. How can we get out of here? And when? And who do we get bread from? Those were the desperate questions I was aware of. There was no time for fairy tales.

People disappeared from the ghetto. We heard rumors about people forced into work camps. I imagine that one night a man whispered to my father, "Those work camps are not really labor camps where you dig ditches or build barracks. People are killed there. Once you go in, you never come out."

During the day, Germans would bark through bullhorns from their cars, commanding certain groups of people to gather on the street or to meet inside a church or courthouse. They didn't say why. These terrorizing *aktionen*, as they were called, were like cattle round-ups. A typical *aktion* order would be, "All men between the ages of sixteen and thirty come to the courthouse at ten tomorrow morning!" Or a voice yelled, "All women with children under the age of twelve, meet on the street *now! Jetzt!*" Following the pronouncements, the Gestapo would march into homes with their boots stomping in search of those who did not obey. Children and older people were wanted the most. By eliminating children, the Nazis intended to permanently end the next generation of Jews.

"Where are you? You stopped talking," Angela interrupted my slide into the past and summoned me from the ghetto back to the couch. I was glad to be back, but I also felt sad to leave the past, where my whole family was still alive.

"Sorry, I was just thinking."

"What were you thinking?"

"Nothing. Can you read me a story now?"

"OK. You have a choice. Do you want to hear Pushkin, the Brothers Grimm, or Hans Christian Anderson?"

I picked the Brothers Grimm. She got up from the couch, saying, "I'll be right back." She returned with her laptop, onto which she had downloaded the story "Little Brother and Little Sister." She started to read in her soothing voice:

"Little brother took his little sister by the hand and said, 'Since our mother died, we have not had a single good hour. Our stepmother beats us every day. Hard, leftover crusts of bread are our food. The little dog under the table is better off, for she often throws it a good morsel. God have mercy, if our mother were to know about this. Come, let us go away together into the wide world.' They walked the whole day over meadows, fields, and stones…"

Having heard the beginning, I fell asleep, knowing that at the end of the story, some magical power would appear to transform the curse into something wonderful and allow brother and sister to live happily ever after. Don't all fairy tales end this way?

I awoke to Angela admonishing me, teasingly. "You fell asleep. I read the whole story, and you didn't even hear it!"

"I know, but I think I figured out the ending." I smiled. "Thanks. I liked the way you read to me." I felt calmed by the heat of her body and the softness of her voice. After some silence, I asked, "Do you like cowboy movies?"

"Not particularly. Why?"

"I grew up with them. I loved to watch them." I told her how it all started. One Saturday afternoon, a few months after my arrival, I passed by a movie theater with the words "Hopalong Cassidy" on the marquee. On the wall poster, I saw a cowboy galloping on a horse. The movie looked exciting to me. But I didn't know what "Hopalong Cassidy" meant. I returned to the studio apartment where I lived with my mother and got the English-to-Polish and English-to-English dictionaries. I couldn't find "hopalong" but I found "hop," which translated to "bounce" or "to leap" in Polish. The "along" meant "to the side" or "next to." I couldn't find "Cassidy" in either dictionary. Although I couldn't tell from the title what the movie was about, I thought it would be fun to see. It was the first movie I ever saw of any kind, and Hopalong became the first of my cowboy heroes. All the heroes wore white hats, except Hopalong, who wore a black hat, but his clothes and gun handles were all white.

I was also drawn to Roy Rogers. He wore a white Stetson hat with a silver headband, rode his golden palomino named Trigger, and always left a cloud of dust behind him. Rogers had a handsome face and comforting smile. I was enthralled that he rescued so many people he didn't even know. He punched the bad guys, saved the scared woman or the outnumbered man from getting shot, and carried a boy on his horse to safety. Sometimes he sang and even yodeled as he rode on his horse. The song I remember was "Tumbling Tumbleweed," whose soothing melody comforted me.

Then there was the masked cowboy with the hidden identity that I listened to on the radio Saturday mornings. *The Lone Ranger*'s usual opening announcement was:

"A fiery horse with the speed of light, a cloud of dust, and a hearty 'Hi-Yo, Silver, away!' The Lone Ranger!" In my apartment, I'd lower the volume and put my ears close to the radio, so I'd have privacy with the Ranger and his Indian partner, Tonto. The specific reasons for his disguise were a mystery to me, but his need to hide made me feel close to him.

I kidded Angela. "You think the Lone Ranger was really a Jew in disguise?"

"Oh, please!"

After a pause, she said, "The cowboys *were* your heroes. The good guys in white hats protected people and got rid of the bad guys. That is a fairy tale, no?" Angela put into words my own simultaneous revelation that I did have my own fairy tales! I felt deeply grateful for this most surprising gift, which seemed to appear out of nowhere. Still, I felt sadness that when I was a child, I had no memory of anyone reading to me in the comfort of my own bed.

We sat in silence watching the logs burn and crackle with flying sparks. I looked up at the dark, gray ceiling and imagined a movie screen. I asked, "Can I tell you a real fairy tale that I just made up?"

"A *real* fairy tale? OK."

"Once upon a time, there lived three extraordinary, heroic warriors in different parts of America. They were strong and good and battled evil people to protect the innocent. They helped people no matter who they were, Christian or Jew. They were cowboys who rode on special horses with unusual strengths. They were fast on the draw, unmatched by any other human. Although they were strangers, they had heard of each other's reputation. Their names were Hopalong Cassidy, the Lone Ranger, and Roy Rogers. Far from where they lived and in the future of their own time, a worldwide war was started by a man named Hitler. In the year 1939, he and his Nazi soldiers attacked many countries. Their evil ideas ripped through the world like tsunamis drowning innocent people. He captured many countries and terrorized and tortured all kinds of people. Hitler's big mission was to eradicate the Jewish people, whom he hated with a passion.

"In Poland, one of the countries the Germans invaded, there lived a four-year-old boy who was loved very much by his mother and father. Before this war, they were a happy family. His father was well liked and respected by all the people who knew him, Catholics and Jews. But at the age of thirty-two, the father was captured by the Gestapo. They pushed him with machine guns, along with tens of others, into a cattle car. This train was going to go to a monstrous place called Belzec. Belzec was a camp that was especially designed to kill Jews by gas and then to cremate them by the thousands. No one ever escaped. Back in America, Roy Rogers heard of the little boy who was about to lose his father. He summoned the other well-known cowboys, Hopalong Cassidy and the Lone Ranger. They met for the first time in a saloon someplace in the West to discuss the dire situation of the four-year-old boy in Poland. They decided to combine their strengths and help him. They had extraordinary, magical powers that enabled them to travel across time, into the future and back, and across faraway places.

"The three warriors transported themselves to the year 1942, to Stanisławów, Poland, where the train that was carrying his father had departed. They waited on top of a ridge in the countryside, where the tracks curved, and the train had to slow down. As the train approached, they sprung out of their cover and rode alongside it, Roy Rogers on the left and Cassidy and the Ranger on the right. They signaled the engineer to stop. He refused, and pulled his gun out to shoot the cowboys. But the Ranger was quicker and shot him while riding his horse. The train picked up speed and was about to run wild without any driver. Rogers rode close to the train, stood up on his saddle, jumped off his horse onto the locomotive, and quickly put the brakes on. When the train squealed to a stop, other guards began to shoot, but the cowboys were faster and sharper and made the train safe for the people inside.

"Once the guns were silenced, the Ranger, Roy, and Hopalong slid open the doors of the cattle cars and let all the people out. Men and women jumped out of the train like freed animals. Most were confused as to where to go, what direction to flee. Some ran straight into the countryside. Others ran in groups, trying to figure out their next move to safety. Everyone was grateful for the miracle that had saved them from sure death, the miracle pulled off by these very odd-looking men on horses. As the people scattered, the cowboys singled out one man, who they circled with their horses. That person was the little Polish boy's father. Roy Rogers extended his hand and pulled the father up onto his beautiful palomino so he could sit behind him. All three warriors then galloped back to the father's town to reunite him with his son.

The father hugged his son and his wife. The reunion was a miracle that he didn't expect in his wildest dreams. The cowboys then took the boy, his mother, and his father on their horses and rode quickly out of town so the Germans couldn't catch them. They came to a farmhouse owned by a kind, very brave young Christian Polish couple and asked them to shelter the whole family until the war ended. The couple agreed and welcomed the boy and his parents. Before the parents could turn around to express their deep gratitude, the three warriors rode off into the distance, leaving a cloud of dust behind them. The boy and his parents lived happily ever after. The end."

Angela lay in silence. I heard her whisper, "That's some fairy tale. I don't know what to say." She pulled me over and let my head lie on her chest. My mind was quiet and friendly, for now.

The Glass Wall

I sat on a beach at a Caribbean resort and watched a woman lying on a large, blue towel with her arms and legs spread out so the sun could touch her all over. I assumed she was French because she was naked, except for the string bottom and a black band wrapped around her right ankle. I wondered if her nipples, pointed directly at the sun, were sunscreen-protected. She was beautiful, and she looked like she was younger than thirty. Her skin gleamed from oils she had applied, and her full mouth reminded me of the French actress Brigitte Bardot.

A few confident men approached her, trying to start something, but none were welcomed to stay. It was a show. No man interested her enough to raise her head. I tried to listen for their pick-up lines, but the persistent wind blowing from the sea muffled their voices. I was impressed by her imperial posture, which surrendered only to the sun and to no human.

I had come alone to Barbados to chill out after a stressful divorce. It was February, and I was fifty years old and living in New Jersey, with two kids in high school.

Lunch was self-service. It was my luck that I entered the dining room at the time when she was picking out her food at the counter. I walked over to line up behind her. I strained to keep my eyes on the assortment of salad and fruit platters sitting on ice.

"The mango salad looks great," I said casually, not even looking at her. "Yes," she answered. "I had it yesterday. Try it." We loaded up our trays. I took a couple of deep breaths, then asked, "Do you mind if I sit with you for lunch?"

"If you like," she said coolly, and pointed her head to an empty table. I figured there were too many years between us for me to threaten her isolation.

She had a slight French accent, so I made a comment about her being used to better cuisine in France. "Oh, but it's OK here," she said. "I am not fussy." She ate very properly, cutting the chunks of fruit with a knife. "Where are you from?" she said, looking up to ask me.

"I'm from New York City."

"But you have an accent."

I always get nervous when my accent is detected. I was reluctant to tell my history.

"Very few people notice it; I am surprised you did," I replied.

"Well, I speak several languages, and I studied theater and speech. So, where were you born?" she persisted.

"In Poland," I answered.

"You're Polish?" she said with surprise.

"No, I am Jewish, born in Poland."

"Oh, so you came to America before or after the war?"

"After. I was eleven," I answered.

I felt put on the spot, about to be exposed. The next question would usually be, "So, how and where did you survive the war?"

I tried to take control, so I quickly asked, "And you, where were you born?"

"Actually, I was born in a town near Munich, called Ulm," she said. "I met my husband, who is French, at the university in Paris." When she married, she moved to Paris to be with him. But they had separated about six months ago.

"*Ich spreche ein bisschen Deutsch,*" I said, surprising her.

"*Ach*, you speak German!" she responded with a smile. "Where did you learn it?"

"Don't ask to me to say anything in German because that's about all I remember. I lived three years in Munich after the war. And I haven't spoken German since." I continued, "So, your parents... they are German?"

"Yes." Then she paused and focused on her papaya and mango salad.

For a few minutes, we ate our lunch in silence. A heightened tension composed of curiosity and the expectation of something dangerous descended on us. While I had sexual feelings, I doubted her interest, as I was so much older. Her background dominated my suspicious thoughts.

I was calculating how old she was and how old her father would have been during the war—was he in the army? A Nazi? Did he shoot Jews? What was she thinking?

She broke the silence. "I hope I am not too intrusive, but were you a child during the war in Poland?"

"Yes," I said.

There was something about her curiosity that made me feel safe and drew me to her. I had wondered what it would be like to talk to a German about my Holocaust experience, and I actually felt like telling her about myself. She was of the first generation of children born to fathers who fought for the Nazis. I sensed that I was the first Jew she would have talked to about the war.

I must have stammered a bit when I asked if she would like to take a walk on the beach. "Yes, that would be nice, but later," she said.

We met at four o'clock and began our stroll along the water's edge. Barbara wore a simple, white, short-sleeved T-shirt and a yellow, flowered sarong wrapped around her with a knot at the waist. She still had that black band around her ankle. A yellow band held her thick, wavy, brown hair straight up and it looked like she had a bouquet of loose, spring flowers on her head, exposing a high forehead and Nordic features. Her attitude and hair made her look taller than she was. Standing next to her, I realized she was shorter than me.

The sun began to descend on the horizon, painting the beach in warm hues of red and gold. The water calmed down, and the shallow waves were just whispers rolling over the sand. The beach was near empty, except for a few boys tossing a volleyball around.

We strolled without talking. I kicked the sea, watching it splash her legs as she laughed and leapt to escape the water.

"You know, my generation has a big interest in the Holocaust," she started. "More than our elders. A couple of years ago, I saw a TV series called *Holocaust*. Do you know it?"

"Was that the one with Meryl Streep?" I asked.

"Yes. I remember I watched it with my friends. That was the first time I really heard the word 'holocaust' refer to the persecution of Jews."

"What did people call it before?"

"There is a German word, *Judenverfolgung*. It means the persecution of Jews. Until that movie, that's what the Germans called the Holocaust."

"Persecution? Not killing?"

"You know, the movie made the Holocaust real. It was about the life of a normal Jewish family with children who were first persecuted and then sent to a concentration camp." She ignored the question but didn't get ruffled. Her composure made me feel safe to reveal myself. I felt bad about being so confrontational.

She explained that the movie enabled the Germans to humanize everyone involved in the Holocaust. They began to discuss the events more openly and meaningfully. "Before the movie," she went on, "the Germans discussed the war more in terms of statistics: were there 6 million or 5.6 million Jews who died? But my generation has a different attitude toward the Holocaust than our elders," she said.

"How?"

"Well, we talk about it, write about it, build memorials. The movie made our generation curious. Young people began to ask what their parents did during the war."

"Did you?"

"In my house, there is a wall of silence about those years. We are not allowed to ask any questions of my father or mother. Frankly, I get very emotional about it when I think of what the Germans did."

"Your father was in the army?" I asked softly.

"Yes, of course! All the men had to be. He had to be. He was thirty-nine when I was born in 1954. I only heard a brief history about my father from my grandmother. He fought in Czechoslovakia, then in the first invasion of Poland, and finally the Russian front. He was lucky to escape the Russian counterattack and the terrible winter and disease there. The German soldiers were starving and dying from typhus, my grandmother said. He had been married and returned home to find his first wife living with a boyfriend in their house. He was a broken man by the time the war ended. And then the betrayal really tore his soul." She wiped her eyes with the back of her hand. "He met my mother a couple years after the war."

I could only say, "I'm sorry."

"I wish my father would talk to me about his past. But we are forbidden from asking any questions." She slipped her sunglasses from her forehead to cover her eyes, and she looked down at the sand. I felt for her, having to carry the burden of not knowing what her father might have done in the war. I imagine she wondered with dread whether her father committed any atrocities. Did he shoot women and children and then push them into a mass grave? Was he in the Gestapo? Or did he just fight enemy soldiers?

Trying to comfort her, I said, "I guess this heavy silence makes you imagine all kinds of things. Would it have been better for him to be less mysterious?"

"I suppose so," she reflected, and turned to me. "Does *your* family talk about your past?"

"Actually, my mother does, but only if I bring it up. I don't recall her initiating much. She has a sharp memory, but she wants to protect me. So, there is a wall of silence with my mother, too. But she welcomes my questions."

"How about your father?" she asked.

"He was killed. Except for my mother's brother and a cousin, all of my family was killed." (I hesitated to use the word *murdered* in front of her).

"How did you survive?"

I told her about the ghetto in my hometown, Stanisławów, and how my father obtained Christian identity papers; how my mother and grandmother and I escaped the ghetto and hid our identity; how a Polish landlady, probably for a reward of a kilo of flour, called the Gestapo on my grandmother; how my father was betrayed by a school friend; and how both were shipped to the Belzec concentration camp, where they died (I resisted saying that they were gassed). I told her how my mother placed me in a convent outside Warsaw for two years, from age six to eight. And then how smart and gutsy she was to get a job as a nanny with a Gestapo family in Warsaw.

"When I hear your story, I get very upset. I get confused. Maybe I feel guilty. I don't know. How could Germans have done such horrible things?" she asked. She hesitated and then went on. "I read *Night* by Elie Wiesel. I couldn't sleep for days. I felt terrible about what my people did. I could only speak with my friends about all of this. I was afraid to speak to anyone my parents' age."

The sun changed to deeper red and orange and began its descent behind the edge of the sea. Once it touched the horizon, it appeared to fall at a faster rate, in staccato movements. We stopped talking and sat on the cool sand to watch this miracle.

When it was time to return to our rooms, I walked her to the lobby; she said goodnight and gave me a kiss on the cheek.

"Oh, by the way, what's your room number?" I asked.

"*Achtunddreissig,*" she said, grinning, and waited to see if I got it.

"*Danke.* Number thirty-eight. OK." I said.

In my room, after a late dinner alone, I lay in bed thinking about my afternoon with Barbara. Our conversation had left me so emotionally charged that I felt like I was rewinding a movie over and over again. I couldn't calm my mind and felt as if drunken monkeys were hopping all over the trees. I needed to talk to her. I dialed her room.

"Did I wake you?"

"No, not at all."

"I need to talk to you. I want to say that I had a really nice day with you and wondered if you are OK with our talks?"

"*Ja, ja.*" I was amused by her German seeping in. "I am. But you called me. Are you OK with it?"

"Well, yes, I am. I guess so. I feel a little unnerved. This is the first time I have had a conversation with a German." Who is a beautiful woman, I thought but didn't say. I didn't think I would feel as comfortable speaking about the Holocaust with a man, even one as young as she, much less one her father's age. Men were too close to the soldiers. After all, women were not in the army. But talking with Barbara was exciting. I felt that something transformative could develop out of this new experience.

"You mean like talking to the enemy?" she asked.

"You're not the enemy."

"*Ja*, but the Germans of my father's generation were, no?"

"It may seem strange to you," I responded quietly, "but I have more hostility toward Poles than Germans. The Germans were the originators of the Holocaust, and I did see them as evil enemies. But it was the Polish people, my neighbors and friends, who betrayed us. It's more personal with Poles, if you can understand. The Germans built the camps in Poland and Ukraine because they knew they would have a cheering and sympathetic population there to help them with the killings. Still, I have to say, there were some extraordinary Poles who risked their lives to save Jews. The nuns and priest in the convent saved my life." I stopped short. "Am I upsetting you?" I asked. "I get worked up about these things. That's all I need to say."

"No, you are not. Oh, maybe a little, yes. *Ach*, it gets complicated for me. There is shame, guilt, and all kinds of messy feelings to struggle with. I do feel some responsibility, not for myself but for my elders. You are the first Jew I have spoken to about any of these things. It's all new to me. So, I am still sorting out how it is for me. But I feel safe with you. Actually, I am surprised I can talk to you as much as I have."

We paused to calm the agitation we both felt. We acknowledged to each other that because of my history and our mutual curiosity, we had formed a quick connection. I remember reflecting with her that it was weird to talk about these dark things on a Caribbean island with clear, blue skies. Then we spoke about the day like any two normal people.

I must have fallen asleep while talking because I woke up late at night with the phone still by my ear. The clock said three-thirty. The line was not dead. So, I asked timidly, "Hello? Are you there?"

And in the stillness of the night, a sleepy, sweet voice answered, "Yes, I am still here."

"God, I am sorry, what happened?"

"You fell asleep in the middle of a sentence and began to snore. I didn't want you to wake up alone," she responded softly.

"So, you hung on all these hours? Wow. I don't know what to say."

"I fell asleep, too, but I held onto the phone. Well, let's say goodnight, all right?" she asked.

The next day, we decided to have dinner outside the resort. Our talks continued to be so engaging that we spent most of the next four days together, becoming closer and deepening our friendship. One day, I took her sailing on a sixteen-foot catamaran. It had a jib and a mainsail, so the wind sliced the boat through the warm sea at high speeds. We screamed and laughed as the water sprayed us from all directions. On the way back, as we approached the shore, a wave caught the boat broadside and knocked us over. The water was so shallow that we were able to stand. With our life jackets still on, we lay on our backs laughing and letting the waves wash over us. She held my hand while the boat lay on its side, the sails slapping the top of the water.

One evening, we went dancing to a band playing swing. Since we were in that transitory space of being friends with just a hint of romance, we were awkward with each other. Good dancing requires surrender to the rhythm. But since we didn't know whether to surrender to each other, how could we surrender to the rhythm? We were particularly stiff when the band played slow pieces. She surprised me, given her age, when she told me she liked big bands from the '40s like those led by Glenn Miller and Jimmy Dorsey. We danced close, but our bodies did not touch. Nevertheless, I was close enough to smell the fresh aroma radiating from her neck and shoulders. It aroused in me youthful spirits and joyful memories. I saw myself at fifteen, kissing a curly-haired girl in the movies for the first time. The kiss felt forbidden and exciting. I smiled to myself. I tried to press Barbara gently to me, but she was firm in keeping her distance.

On the last night at the resort, Barbara asked me to come to her room to celebrate our goodbye. We sat on a pink velvet couch with a bottle of white wine I had bought in town.

I kissed her mouth and felt a stirring in her. I kissed her neck, which made her lift her chin, further exposing herself to me. With my lips, I caressed her neck and shoulders. Her sweet, natural scent, like a summer peach, aroused me. I sniffed her like an animal. She began to laugh and then breathe more heavily. When she kissed me, she held my head gently with both hands and skimmed my lips with her tongue.

During a pause, she began to cry and told me about her husband's infidelities. She couldn't tolerate the last one, so she told him to get out. She excused herself and hurried into the bathroom to compose her emotions. I could hear her blowing her nose. When she returned, she apologized for crying. I told her that she didn't need to apologize, and she continued to tell me about her husband's other affairs.

"You are the first person I am kissing after nine years of marriage," she told me. "I was not a virgin bride, but I was very young. I was twenty when I got married."

I stroked almost every part of her body. We now sat opposite each other on the couch with her legs wrapped around my waist. I stroked her leg from the ankle up and felt the softness of her inner thigh. I heard her enjoying my hands. Then we kissed, and I caressed her back as her breast filled my other hand. She slipped her hand on my chest with a touch so gentle my body shivered. We changed positions in a harmonious rhythm that we hadn't found on the dance floor. With smooth movements, we kissed, we hugged, and we felt each other. That's how we made love on the couch that last night, without touching each other's sexual parts ("Let's wait. I am not ready yet, OK?" she asked.)

Late in the evening, I looked into her eyes so closely that our noses touched. "I am scared," I whispered.

"Of what?" she asked, just as quietly.

"Of not having you. Of losing you," I answered.

Her eyes focused on mine, and I saw in them a clear, blue, mountain spring flowing directly toward me. She startled me. The water was so clear that I saw glistening pebbles covering the bottom of her stream.

"I am afraid, too," she said. And she kissed my wet eyes, her tongue licking the tears off my cheeks. "I wonder why."

"Because we both know this is temporary." I could only whisper the words.

In the early morning, before I went to my room to pack, we made plans to talk on the phone, and she invited me to visit her in Paris.

Over the next two months, from our home cities, we spoke several times a week. Each time I dialed, I thought I was dialing a secret code that would unlock the door to my happiness. My magnetic attraction to Barbara was phantasmal. It was as if the relationship would uncover every cloud's silver lining and restore the love I lost as a child.

I made plans to fly to Paris in the magical month of April, about two months after we met. On my tape, I heard Ella Fitzgerald and Louis Armstrong singing, "April in Paris... chestnuts and blossoms... I never knew my heart could sing..."

I booked a Thursday night flight out of New York that would arrive in Paris early Friday morning; I'd return late Sunday night. I arrived at the American Airlines counter with my documents. I showed the agent my passport and my tickets. She looked up and said, "Where is your visa?"

"I wasn't told anything about a visa. I have my passport but no visa."

"Then you'll need to get one at the French consulate."

"I can't. I changed my work schedule. I arranged a short weekend. People are waiting for me in Paris."

She wouldn't let me board. I felt desperate, and my anger was rising. I thought there must be some way to get onboard. I demanded to speak to her supervisor. She paged him, and I spoke to him on the phone. I explained the situation to him and asked if there was some way to enter France without a visa.

"Well, there is a temporary visa you can get. But it's only for forty-eight hours. You'll have to get it at the Paris immigration office."

I was so relieved. "OK. That's fine. Why didn't anyone tell me this in the first place?"

I landed in Paris early in the morning. I was told to sit in the waiting area by the immigration offices, which were still closed. A thick glass wall contained the area. At eight-thirty, a tall, civilian Frenchman approached me and asked if I was the one waiting for a temporary visa. He told me to wait. About fifteen minutes later, he returned and said that I could have a visa, but it would cost forty-five francs. I found the situation amusing. The bureaucrat then asked me for the francs. I told him I only had dollars. He said he couldn't take dollars, only francs.

"But I don't have francs. I just got here."

"Well, then you can't get the visa." I was hoping this was just dry humor. My smile disappeared when I saw his serious expression. I looked around and saw a bank across the hall. I asked him if I could get change at the bank. He refused permission, saying that the bank was in French territory and I didn't have a visa.

"How will I get francs then? Do I have to return to the U.S. to get them? Is there no way I can cross to the bank!?"

It was then that I saw Barbara looking at us through the glass wall. She was smiling and waving at me. I wanted to run out and hug her. I asked if he could let me through to say hello, but he refused. Instead, he left me staring at Barbara through the wall.

He returned to inform me there was actually a way I could get change: I had to be accompanied by a *gendarme*.

In a few minutes, two women dressed in uniforms appeared with guns on their hips. They were amused, and one was laughing. I was wondering what Barbara was thinking. With one on either side of me, we marched onto French soil and into the bank. I felt like James Bond. People were looking at me as if I were some important and wealthy man. The *gendarmes* took off their hats and flung their blond hair free, laughing at their escort duty.

Once I got my visa, I walked out of the glass cage and hugged Barbara, whose scent immediately stirred memories of Barbados. I checked into my hotel while Barbara, as she had warned me, went to work.

Worried thoughts about Barbara muffled my excitement about being in Paris. I tried to stay active. I went to the Louvre to see Mona Lisa, who was smaller than I thought; she was protected by so many layers of Plexiglas that she lost her appeal. In the early afternoon, I visited the church of Sainte-Chapelle, where I sat in a pew, listening to the magic of Vivaldi's "Four Seasons." With heavy eyes, I searched for meaning in the stained glass windows depicting the Old and New Testaments. I thought about my upcoming conversations with Barbara. I felt restless and unable to relax.

At dinner that night, she said, "I've been thinking about our age difference. I know this is a sensitive topic, but I frankly have never been attracted to anyone your age. I didn't know how it would feel, how it would be. I never thought I would have sexual feelings for someone your age. The oldest man I have been out with was thirty. Actually, it's been liberating with you. I like you and had fun with you. But I haven't gotten totally used to it yet."

She was being honest, and her hesitations were understandable. After all, I hadn't thought that she'd be interested in me when I first saw her on the beach. But we'd been so romantic in Barbados; to hear her backpedaling was painful. I felt self-conscious, and wanted to check my thinning hair. I straightened my posture in the chair.

"You feel self-conscious being with me in public?" I asked nervously.

"No, no. It's just that I have to get accustomed to it."

"Do you think we have a future together?"

"Oh, I haven't thought that far. I try just to think about the present."

"How can you think of age and not think about the future?" I asked, gazing at her.

"I think the future is closer to you than to me."

That's true, I thought. For me, one year is a long time. For her, maybe a week. Still, I didn't like her saying it. And I felt there was something else going on behind her hesitation.

"Did you tell your parents about me at all?"

"I told them about your age and that you are an American."

"No, you know what I mean."

"I told you, in my house, no one speaks about the war."

"I am thinking about my religion, not the war." My body stiffened.

"OK. I... I... didn't tell them directly you are Jewish. They somehow assumed that you were because I told them you were born in Poland." After a tense pause, she began, "Look, I have to tell you something very difficult. I really like you very much. I didn't know I could be attracted to you as much as I am. We have had such wonderful times and unexpected talks. It's not about me being German and you, Jewish. It's the ordinary things that are a problem. I want babies. You already have two, and you don't want any more. My husband never wanted children. But now I do. I really do." Her eyes became wet.

I understood, of course. She was twenty-nine. It's natural to want children. I expected it, too. Didn't I tell her that night in Barbados that I feared we would end? Yet now I was numbed by the depth of the sadness that overcame me. This was goodbye. I was shaken. I saw her hand move across the table, but I was so tense that I couldn't move my hand toward hers. I thought I should. I wanted to.

I noticed that she was stronger and braver than me. Across from me she was experiencing the goodbye of separation, tearfully explaining herself, while I sat helpless, as if I were observing from above the painful discussion we were having. My mind was flooded with thoughts, and I couldn't be reasonable. That bothered me. Even worse, it shamed me. Why was she able to face the reality, while I was unnerved by it?

On the street outside the restaurant, we said goodbye, hugging each other. It was only when my head was on her shoulders during our hug, when she couldn't see me, that my tears appeared. "We'll talk," I whispered. She nodded her head. We parted in opposite directions. For a moment, I watched her hurry away. My mind fogged over as I tried to find my way back to the hotel.

In twenty-five years, I have not forgotten Barbara. The memories of us are as clear as the blue stream that flowed in her eyes. Over the years, the most difficult challenge for me was to remember the wonderful romance with Barbara while simultaneously tolerating the terrible pain that came with that loss. I have always appreciated the unique dimension of our relationship, the intimacy of which revolved around the Holocaust. While I was history's victim, she, too, suffered the burden of the destructive forces that her people unleashed on the world.

When I think back to our weekend in Paris, I always see Barbara, smiling and waving at me from the other side of the glass wall, as I listened to the immigration officer's harsh but prescient words: "You can't go through."

The Pond

During the best part of the day, I sat on my beach chair with the sun setting behind me, watching people wade through the water, as parents began to gather their children and their plastic buckets, shovels, and colored cars.

In front of me, I saw a father struggling to fit blue ear-plugs into his little boy's ears. First the right ear, which took several minutes, then turning the boy, he did the left. The boy, who I thought would be hurting or irritated, had a blank expression, passively allowing the father to plug his ears, as if this procedure were only too familiar to him. The father looked confident and patient.

The little boy, perhaps eight, was dressed in a blue shirt and brown shorts. His round, black eyes focused on something far away that I could not find. He held a red fire truck in his left hand. His mother, a middle-aged woman, watched this procedure with her back to me.

The sun cast the mother's shadow on the boy. It resembled a rounded turtle with thick legs and a short neck. Her head was bent over, as if she had emerged temporarily out of her shell to observe this routine event. Her hands rested on her waist like they were too heavy to simply hang. An elderly bald man with patches of gray hair on both sides of his head joined the observers. I assumed he was the grandfather. He had a protruding, strong nose and, like his daughter, simply gazed at the ear plugging.

When the father had finished with his boy, the grandfather motioned for the couple to go swimming, pointing his hand toward the ocean. It was impossible to hear what they were saying above the roar of the wind and surf. Not to worry, he seemed to gesture, he would watch the boy. The parents looked grateful and wandered off to take a dip in the ocean.

The little boy began to walk slowly from right to left, parallel with the water. In front of him, another boy, slightly older and wiry, was busy running to and from the water, filling the hole he had dug with his blue shovel. He looked determined and proud to complete his project—a three-foot-wide pond. After emptying a bucket of water, he carefully pressed the sand around the pond to secure its wall. He had light brown hair and brown eyes, and his movements were purposeful and focused, hurrying to complete his work before the tide rolled in.

The boy in blue, followed by his grandfather, watched the industrious boy and then slowly stepped into the hole, obviously feeling good that he found a pond in the middle of the beach. At first, he just stood in the water, while the older boy kept filling up the pool. Then he dropped down and sat in the water that had been warmed by the sun and sand. Some of the water spilled out. The builder was surprised by this uninvited stranger who now occupied his pool. The builder looked up to the grandfather, pleading for some help. The grandfather looking proudly at his grandson, ignored the boy's plea.

The older boy kept running to the ocean, filling his can, and pouring fresh water into the pool. Each time he refilled the pool, he would look up to the grandfather with a plea to stop this intrusion. The man continued to be oblivious to the situation, focusing only on the pride of his family line. The boy in blue, bored with watching, began to use his truck to empty the pool. As the builder brought water in, the boy spilled water out.

The builder stopped and gave the grandfather a long, frustrated look. With open hands, he pleaded, "What is going on here? Do something." But the grandfather, so proud of his boy's accomplishment, paid no attention. This cycle continued until the blue boy stood up, his fire truck still in his hand, dripping with water. He stepped out of the pond and looked around for his next adventure. The builder now began to restore his damaged pool.

Meanwhile, the parents returned, staring proudly at their son. The mother smiling and beaming with pride, said to the grandfather, "Isn't he cute? Isn't he wonderful?" The boy tripped and fell. His father dutifully helped him up and patted him on his back. "OK, go on," his father encouraged and then returned to his chair.

The grandmother came along with two beach chairs. The family sat down to watch the show. The boy was free to do whatever his imagination desired. Strangely, no one in his family threw a ball to him, wrestled with him, chased him, or tickled him. It appeared to me that his family viewed the entire beach as their son's playground. They assumed that the beach would provide the entertainment and the friends that he needed.

He ventured to a castle that several children were constructing. He joined them, watched a little, and then placed his red truck on the highest point of the castle and pressed down. The parapet, along with some of the walls, crumbled. The children looked shocked. Noticing that adults were watching, they were tentative and diplomatic in their defense. One of the children gently lifted the truck and placed it by the boy's feet, resuming repair of the damage.

The family continued to observe with pride and to smile at their son's activity from afar. The sun retreated, darkening the water and flooding the beach with deep red colors. Its departure was a foreboding, like the silence that precedes a coming storm. The boy in blue searched the beach, desperate to find children to play with. But he saw only the backs of children and their parents leaving the beach, carrying their toys, coolers, and bags of various shapes and colors.

With the ocean calmed and the wind slowed, he could now hear everything, but there was little to hear, except the sound of silence. He found himself in stillness, standing in a barren desert. I looked on, observing a troubled expression transform his face. I sensed a perilous panic in him. In contrast to the earlier, aimless meandering, he now seemed desperate to touch someone. With his back to the ocean, he scanned the beach once more from right to left, starting with his family, whom he noticed but did not see. They were still smiling, consumed by parental pride that blinded them to the desperation of their child. They looked past the boy, rather than inside him. The boy turned his head away, as if they were not there. His eyes landed on me, and for a moment, I thought he would approach me. I would have welcomed him, but I was frightened by his painful aloneness, which was only too familiar within me. Lying on my lounge chair with my sunglasses hiding my eyes, I felt torn and did not know what to do. Although he was desperate for human contact, even from a stranger, he may have sensed my fears. I think he saw me looking at him, but his eyes kept moving past me. I was relieved, yet felt helpless, not knowing what to do. There was no one beyond me but an empty beach.

After a moment of stillness, having completed his scan, he turned toward the water. With renewed purpose, he chased the swash into the ocean as it retreaded from the beach. Suddenly the parents' dreamy smiles became looks of alarm. I watched them chase their son into the now menacing sea.

Autumn Leaves

W hen I sleep with Aline, I like to wrap my arms around her slender body and find her hand. Her fingers automatically wrap around my finger, like a baby who wraps her hand around someone's finger, not caring if the person is familiar or a stranger.

But Aline, who has already pressed her back toward me, knows who I am. In the morning, she says that while a baby may wrap its hand around anyone's, she would only do this for me.

I thought she must be awake, but no, I could tell by her hoarse breathing sounds that she was asleep. Her response was a measure of how tender she felt toward me. And how warm my mind and body felt with her.

My mother and father had once placed their fingers in my hand while I slept in my crib and smiled with pride at my grip. My mother was nineteen, my father twenty-five when I was born in Poland, where I once had a safe home. But here, I am old, an unimagined seventy-five, placing my finger into the hand of a woman near my age.

When I was younger, I thought that when a man reaches sixty, he is done and should be placed in a home, too frail to live on his own. Yet, at seventy-five, I don't feel any particular age, young or old, having slipped off the age dimension.

I hold Aline with tenderness, enjoying the closeness that comes from touching, laughing, and talking with the woman I love. And sometimes, in the morning, in our underwear, we dance the foxtrot to Miles Davis before teeth brushing and coffee.

Painful thoughts intrude during the happiest of times, surprising me like bad, uninvited guests crashing a dinner party. While in bed, feeling the warmth of Aline curled next to me, I think of my town of birth, Stanisławów. I see conquering soldiers wearing black armbands emblazoned with swastikas herding us, along with thousands of other Jews, into the ghetto around which the Germans have built a wall. Like cornered animals, my family struggled with what to do: should they fight or flee? Their minds and bodies were numbed as they beheld the growling attack dogs. The animals were controlled by shouting men in helmets and black boots pointing their bayoneted rifles at them.

At that time, my parents were no longer able to play with me or express affection that comes from love. I felt in their touch and hugs their efforts to protect me from harm's way, but this didn't allay my fears. My parents struggled to survive the Nazi terror and the perils of Polish vigilantes who gave up Jews for money, but more often for eggs or potatoes.

Strange as it seems, when I was a young adult I was not aware that my past had a distinct effect on me, except in some abstract way. It wasn't until my thirties and forties, when I started psychoanalysis, that I began to appreciate the Holocaust's impact on me and could talk about its effects. But it took fifty years to finally feel and see with clarity how deeply the Holocaust had shaped my entire being and my relationships. I became painfully mindful of past images creeping into my life, even when I was happy. During my good times, scary images popped up so dramatically that I felt disoriented. Once, on Martha's Vineyard, I remember feeling good from the heat of the sun, from swimming and drinking delicious wine. At dusk, my friends and I were leaving the beach, walking along a narrow boardwalk. I looked down at my bare feet and saw Nazi boots marching on the street. If I had let myself, I could have heard the echoes of those heels against the sidewalk. I had to struggle to wipe the Nazis out of my mind. And I did, at least that time.

Back in our town ghetto, my father and mother discussed the best option for survival. The Nazis told them they would soon be transported to labor camps. But rumors spread that these places were not camps for labor. Should we flee, or stay as chameleons in disguise? Maybe, my parents thought, if we worship, speak, and act like Polish Christians, the Nazis will lower their guns and not stare at us with that hatred and contempt that permanently branded my mind.

My father obtained Catholic papers for my grandmother, mother, and me. With our new identities and a bribe to the guards at the ghetto gate, we escaped. My father and grandfather, waiting for false documents, needed more time to prepare their escape. But before they were ready to leave, the *aktions* fatally betrayed them, transporting them to death camps. The rumors had been right. There was no labor to be done.

With our Christian papers and new names, my mother played a deadly game of cat-and-mouse with the Gestapo in and out of the city of Lvov. When she sensed that the Germans were closing in, and she had no place to run, Mother placed me in a convent outside Warsaw for safekeeping. She then interviewed in Warsaw with a young Gestapo officer and his wife for a job as a nanny to their three-year-old child. She passed as a childless Polish widow who loved children and got the job. They had a German shepherd who took a liking to her, and she would stroll down the boulevard pushing the baby carriage, with the dog by her side. No one would possibly imagine she was other than she seemed. Like a chameleon, she became someone else.

My mother's courage, street-smart cunning, and luck saved us. Alone, we were left to mourn the loss of all the others. We kept our memories of them alive by telling the story of our family to those brave enough to listen.

After the war, as a young teenager, I lived with my mother in New York. She was an anxious mother, uncomfortable with her emotions and secretive, rarely initiating any talk about my father or the war unless I asked her directly. Her mind was sharp as a reporter's, citing exact dates and street numbers of the places we'd lived. Most of her recollections had to do with factual information. I don't recall her talking much about any emotional experiences.

On my desk is a photograph of my mother taken just before the war, the one she used on her false papers. With her brown eyes, she looks straight at me, striking in her prettiness, almost daring me to talk to her. Her face, with its shiny forehead, appears to have been carved by a sculptor who loved women, endowing her with a sense of sweetness and surprising toughness. She had a nose that a plastic surgeon would have loved. That nose saved her life in the war. Unlike me, with my pronounced nose, she did not look Jewish. She was short but looked taller. As she aged, her face stayed pretty, but her body grew stout and rounded.

When I was in high school, I had asked Mother why she had never remarried.

"Oh, I had a few opportunities, but I didn't want to."

"Why not?"

"There were many reasons. You wouldn't understand."

"Like what?"

She took a deep breath and said, "After the war, there was a man interested in me, but he didn't want to marry me because I had a child. OK?"

Surprised, I tried to clarify my confusion. "There were no others?"

"Look, your father said something to me when I saw him for the last time in that ghetto. It was private. And you're too young to know."

We sat in tense silence. I felt annoyed not knowing this secret, now that I had learned that there was one. She must have sensed my frustration and finally confessed. "When I said goodbye to him, he asked me not to be with another man if anything happened to him. That's all." She rushed off to another room.

I didn't know what to say or think. We never spoke about it again.

I thought about my father's plea for fidelity many times for years to come. I wondered whether my father would ever have demanded this of his twenty-five-year-old wife. I can understand the possessiveness that comes from love, but was he that selfish? No other impressions I got from surviving relatives supported this characterization of my father. On the contrary, he is remembered as kind, intelligent, social, and caretaking. I will never know why she said this to me.

We arrived in America in May of 1949, when I was eleven years old. In July, through a scholarship, she arranged for me to go to summer camp in the Catskills. It was the best thing she could have done for an immigrant who spoke no English. For two months, I was immersed in the language, culture, and most importantly, the sports of my new country. By the time I left camp at the end of August, I spoke English, had made friends, and played softball; third base was my favorite position.

My mother cared for me in every way. Although we were poor, I never felt poor. She gave me a small allowance that I supplemented by working as a delivery boy for cleaners on weekdays and a florist on the weekend. I will never forget the pride I felt from the first money I made. I delivered a suit to an apartment and the man gave me a quarter tip. I ran smiling down the street, holding the quarter in my pocket.

Mother worked hard at jobs she'd never imagined doing. She had grown up in a family of substance in a town where her father, my grandfather, had a successful textile business. We lived in a three-story townhouse built by my grandfather. Mother finished gymnasium, learned piano, and spent one year in dental school in France. For a woman—and a Jew— from Poland to be admitted to a professional school anywhere at that time was simply extraordinary. She quit dental school to return to Poland, so she could marry my father and then have me.

In America, she worked first as a seamstress in a sweat-shop. Later she enrolled in a beauty school, and then found work in a salon styling hair and doing manicures. Tired of laboring long hours, she took a secretarial course at a commercial school. That's when she landed her first white-collar job as a secretary managing an insurance president's appointments and typing his letters. She liked it. It paid well and was in a clean environment. She had a nine-to-five schedule and weekends off.

The odd thing is that until recently, I had not consid-ered how old she was when she arrived in the USA. I realized that, at the age of thirty-four, she had already lived a lifetime of horrors. Now in a strange new country, with English as the common language, she found herself alone, supporting an eleven-year-old son.

She cooked to please me, often making my favorite dish of mushrooms pan-cooked with sour cream, garlic, and onions. I still love that dish, and I can recall its wonderful aroma. She also made pierogi from scratch and filled them with potatoes or plums; the latter had a succulent, sweet juice that seeped out when you pierced one. On weekends, she often cooked a delicious, healing chicken soup from scratch, with dill sprin-kled on top. To this day, in memory of her, I buy dill when I go shopping. I place the dill in a glass of water and squeeze it. I can smell her chicken soup.

There was a blanket over Mother's emotional expression that left me feeling lonely. I would eat dinner with her at our small, round table in the kitchen, and we had little to say to each other. I remember her sitting across from me with a faraway look, nervously picking at her thumb. The tension was so contagious that I often had to finish eating quickly, so I could leave the room. Maybe I also had a blanket covering me. We were unable to reach out to each other. We were both wounded. I didn't know it then. I don't think she did, either.

Because she'd needed to be on perpetual guard in order to survive, she was left with a permanent blanket over her emotional expression, even during happy times. Perhaps she was this way before the war; I'll never know. Feeling lonely throughout my teenage years, I turned to my friends, who I thought of as brothers, and to their parents, some of whom related to me with smiles and unworried conversations about ordinary things in life.

What I valued most about my friends' parents was their absence of anxiety.

When I was of age, I also sought refuge in the basement of our building. The basement had two dim bulbs suspended on a wire from the ceiling, which had large and small crisscrossing pipes. The uneven concrete walls had blotches of white paint, while the floor was concrete and gray. It was cozier in the winter when the air was warm and dry. In the summer, it was hot, humid, and smelled from dampness. But no matter: it was my private nightclub. There was a room that had piles of newspapers and magazines tied together with a rope. I found *Look*, *Time*, and some *Playboy* magazines in the piles. All the girls in these magazines smiled at me. I liked *Playboy* the best, but it was hard to find. In the mid-1950s, it was still new and expensive; it also had, by far, the prettiest girls. The cover girls, especially, and some girls inside gave me great pleasure. In my fantasies, I excited these beautifully shaped women, who responded with moans and groans and pleaded, "Give me more, more" and "Don't stop now!" Sometimes, if I couldn't arouse a particular woman in my fantasy, I just turned the page and found another that I could. I preferred the tall ones with long, shiny legs. I liked both brunettes and blondes. It was all about chemistry. Could we would turn each other on?

I would go down to my club after school or sometimes after dinner, telling my mother that I needed to throw out our newspapers or garbage. Somehow, I kept it all a secret and never had an intruder.

* * *

Aline resumes snoring until I massage her scalp with my fingertips. Her moans sound far away. I stay awake. I think of the many years after my ten-year marriage ended that I had been a romantic drifter, in serial monogamous relationships. But my devotion to my son and daughter remained steadfast, and this connection with them served as an anchor for me. Three years ago my daughter ended my meandering by introducing me to Aline. Within two years we were married in an antique barn, celebrating with dancing, hugging, funny speeches, and laughter. We thanked my daughter with a silver chalice, inscribed "The best matchmaker of the century." All ninety guests cheered, whistled, and clapped. My daughter beamed with pride.

I stay awake; my sad thoughts wander over me like autumn leaves carpeting the grass. I think of Jerzy Kosinski and Primo Levi. After years of breathless running in defiance of their pain, their resilience was spent. Their demons caught up with them and drove them to end their lives.

On my dresser in the shadow of the night, I catch the framed image of my thirty-two-year-old father with his friends in the last year of his life. I feel close to him, even though I don't really remember him. I know that he defied the Nazis. On a cattle car train to Belzec death camp, he broke through a barricaded door and jumped off. Unhurt, he ran to a Christian friend he knew from school for safe haven. But that family felt their duty to the Gestapo took priority over their loyalty to a friend. Father was reported and returned by train to camp. There, he was ordered, along with others, to take his clothes off and clean up in the shower room. Instead of water, gas sprayed from the showerheads. Men in gas masks picked him off the floor and threw him into the oven, along with others. He was cremated, his ashes spread in the sky.

I have outlived my father by forty years, yet I have kept him alive in me through old photographs, fantasies, hearsay, and the memory of others who knew him. While I miss him, I have struggled with my feelings toward Mother. I am grateful and awed by her defiance of the Nazis and her victory in surviving their assaults. Yet I feel guilty for not providing her with more love and closeness. Aline says I am confusing guilt with the regret of not having a more intimate relationship. Indeed, Mother rarely succeeded in removing the blanket over her emotions. We both missed out.

Aline continues to sleep with a comforting pillow between her legs. Her curly, silver-gray hair covers her face as she lies on her side, her hands by her head in prayer position. Her breathing is quiet. Feeling safe, I wrap myself around her and smile with gratitude.

Afterword

My Children's Reflections on How
My Holocaust Experience Affected Them

In 2007 I was invited to participate in a panel discussion entitled "Last Witnesses: Child Survivors of the Holocaust." All four participants had been children during the Holocaust so we were indeed some of the last living witnesses to that period. The panel was videotaped, with the intention of using it as an educational tool. We were asked in advance to discuss various topics, such as how we survived; what role, if any, Christians played in our survival; what had been the effects on our own lives; did we believe in God?; and how our experiences affected our children.

I thought it best for my two children to respond, in their own words, on the topic of how my Holocaust experiences affected them. The following are the letters they sent me in response to my inquiry.

From my daughter

Dad.

I think that my experience of being the child of a Holocaust survivor isn't only about being a daughter of one. I'm the grandchild and niece of one too. So I experience it as how my family survived. When I consider your experience, it makes me sad that you had to go through that as a child. When I consider the experience you had and think about that same thing for Sam, it is unimaginable. But when I think about what you, my grandmother, and uncle had to go through to get us all where we are now, I guess I feel a great sense of pride, for everyone's strength, humility, and thankfulness.

You and I have had many opportunities over the years to discuss this topic together, so I know you are familiar with/can speak about these various conversations. So I guess I will focus on what comes to mind at this point in time....

There was a time during my early childhood when your being a child Holocaust survivor was forefront in my experience of you. Fortunately, that experience has shifted over time, and it has become one aspect of a larger, and largely beautiful, picture of you.

As I contemplate your question to me and Shannon on the occasion of a roundtable on the topic, I am struck by the thought that being a {child} Holocaust survivor (and the daughter of one) is unique to being a "survivor" in other ways (cancer, abuse, etc.) or of other profoundly life-altering experiences (e.g., becoming blind, wheelchair bound, etc.). The people we most admire strive to live life despite their challenges and histories, not as defined by them. That is to say, not to ignore or bury one's past, but not to have their being or their relationships defined by it.

Being a Holocaust survivor, by contrast, is a double-edged sword. In your recent show at St John's, you wanted the portraits to testify to the life-affirming, rebuilding, and resilient qualities of these survivors' lives. Yet at the same time, these conferences and projects carry the concern that these experiences not be left in the past—that they not be forgotten. I would say this unique dance between triumphing and remembering, recovering and recalling, comes from of a sense of obligation to history, to "never forget." The implication being that in the forgetting of history is the threat of repeating it. But as I consider this admonition, I think of a genocide that IS being perpetrated at this very moment in time and wonder how much cause and effect there is between remembering and preventing genocide. I also wonder if this ("never forget") does not make being a Holocaust survivor a uniquely complicated issue in the context of psychoanalysis/therapeutics.

Love,

Jen

Jennifer Alexandra is an architect. She is married with two children.

From my son
THE OBVIOUS

I'm a Jew in a (semi-) functioning democracy with a culture of acceptance. Aside from the rare remarks of a bigot or {an} absent-minded {comment}, I've never experienced racism. And so my father's history, if nothing else, has been a surrogate education providing me with a level of empathy for the diaspora I would not otherwise have. My father's history (which I take on as my own) includes me in a part of history of which, needless to say, is essential to be eternally conscious.

I also think now of my grandfather, who I never met. And I think of my grandmother, whose anxious disposition could only have been exacerbated by the Holocaust. I feel robbed of both, in a way. And I cannot help but wonder what this loss—which I experience both in myself and through my father—has done to shape me. Am I more anxious because of it? Did my parents divorce because of it? Am I not married yet because of it? There are no answers to these questions, but they are most certainly at least ever so slightly, partly correct.

THE HONEST

With the personal connection to the Holocaust described above comes an undesirable responsibility. Many of those unfortunate enough to have experienced the Holocaust will carry it with them perpetually, holding it close enough so as to influence perspectives and conversations. For many this is not a choice but simply a symptom. For others, it is both. I respect the vigilance but I do not wish to "remember" the Holocaust. Had I the choice, I would opt to never have heard of the Holocaust.

Like any violence witnessed, the knowledge of what happened stays with me and taints my perspective. The experience, albeit vicarious, leaves me battered. Why would someone choose to have this information? A rhetorical question, as there is no choice. But while there was no choice in owning this history, there is the choice to be made on whether I will accept this history. And therein lies the brutality of the Holocaust on the next generation. How can we not accept our parents' history? We must accept it, as loving children, as participants in society, as Jews. In the end then, again, it's not much of a choice.

THE HOPEFUL

If one accepts the past, the issues of remorse fall away and one is apt to appreciate the achievements that have come, despite the disadvantages. In this mindset, I am extremely grateful for all I have. My education, my luxuries, my loving parents... they are all the more special knowing how deprived their childhood was—both literally, of course, but also emotionally. It's an impressive and inspiring perspective to have and from within those moments, I'm grateful.

Shannon is an architect.

About the Author

Clemens Loew was born in Poland two years before World War II began. He survived the Holocaust in part by hiding his identity and then by hiding in a convent outside Warsaw. His mother and uncle survived, but the rest of his family was killed.

Following the war, he and his mother stayed in a displaced-person camp and then in Munich, waiting for visas. They arrived in America in 1949, when he was eleven years old, speaking Polish, German, and Hebrew.

He was raised in Manhattan, where he attended public schools.

After obtaining his PhD in clinical psychology at the University of Iowa, he furthered his postgraduate training in New York City. He lives and practices in Manhattan, where he is a psychoanalyst, author, and co-founder of the prominent National Institute for the Psychotherapies. His portraits of child Holocaust survivors, exhibited in the Cathedral of St. John the Divine, in Manhattan, brought him recognition as a photographer. He is married and has children and grandchildren.

Made in the USA
Middletown, DE
10 October 2021

49991427R00111